Contents

The precise type of cottage which proliferated in the North of England throughout the nineteenth century is difficult to identify. For hundreds of years regional differences in climate, available building materials, relative prosperity and density of population had led to the evolution of distinct styles both of settlement and dwelling all over the British Isles. The five types illustrated here merely show the range of rural dwellings of the cheapest kind to be found in early nineteenth-century Britain.

(1) A sod cottage at Jurby, Isle of Man, photographed while still inhabited, in 1897. Smoke can be seen emerging from a wattle chimney over the gable end and no windows are visible – not even the topless and bottomless barrels which centuries ago served as 'wind-eyes' before the widespread use of glass. Whatever the actual age of this building it demonstrates the continuation of a very ancient mode of life right till the dawn of the twentieth century.

(2) In Wales villages were unknown in the sense common in England. The Welsh crofter built his cottage where he had land, and close to the moors where his sheep grazed. Most are now derelict as a result of the arrival of industry and the great land enclosures. This particular example comes from Llanygnog, Montgomeryshire.

1 The coming of mass housing

Scientific Philanthropy (Limited)

'It is the triumph of human intelligence, and the boast of actual society, to be enabled to love one another, not only with the certainty of future benediction, but at a pecuniary profit of almost immediate realisation. "My Lords, Ladies and Gentlemen," cries the modern apostle, not in the wilderness, but in a metropolis of four million and odd souls, "come with me into the highways and byways of this colossal city,— into the suffocating homes of the poor. See how the artisan is lodged, how the sweating brow and horny hand of labour find no rest in comfortless tenements,— how the dwellings generally of working men are a reproach to their employers, who, nevertheless, pay them adequately and heavily. Will you not mend this state of things, especially if you can do so at no cost, and at no risk to yourselves? No money is required of you, my lords, ladies and gentlemen, your practical assistance is neither desired nor desirable; permit me simply to place some of the best-known of your honoured names at the top of this circular, to let the world know that you are supposed to be watching over the conduct of my philanthropic efforts; and money will flow into my coffers,— money with which I can do anything and everything. I want only names—the pillars of limited liability—to raise my superstructure, which, even if it fall, will not fall on you; for, as your purses have not been opened, so their contents will remain intact, and as your honour is now above suspicion so it will then be protected from reproach.'

Part of an attack on unscrupulous house building companies published in 'The Builder' Vol XXV (1877) p 599.

In 1665 a census of the population was taken in Canada, then a French colony. In 1749 the process was repeated in Sweden, in 1790 in the newly formed United States of America, and in 1801 in Britain. From then on the census became a regular decennial event in most Western nations, revealing with startling clarity the enormous demographic changes that had begun to take place within and between them.

The origin of these changes goes back to the fifteenth century when the cumulative growth of scientific knowledge of the physical world began to be widely communicated by means of printing and publishing. The real process of the revolution did not, however, begin until the eighteenth century, when the employment of new inventions in the ex-ploitation of natural resources and the dramatic mechanization of traditional industries such as textiles, began to assume a distinctly novel scale and character. From about 1750 growing literacy in a growing population, scientific enthusiasm and increasing real wealth meant that the apparently meaningless and unrelated experiments of ingenious men were more and more often synthesized into commercially exploitable forms, and this very process of exploitation gave encouragement to those still at work: experiment and innovation became paths to fortune instead of the sport of wealthy amateurs.

It is against the background of a substantially altered attitude to innovation and a growing confidence in the organizational and

(3) Semi-detached housing, which accounted for almost all speculative development between 1919 and 1939, began long before the twentieth century. These cottages at Holbeach Clough, Lincolnshire, date from 1793.

(4) Remaining country cottages in most parts of Britain have become prized as country homes. One in Oxfordshire boasts a Jaguar where sixty years ago a previous tenant and his family committed suicide as a result of hunger. The cottage here represents the image of pre-industrial country life, an image of extraordinary power even today.

(5) The restricted amount of land available around most small harbours led to a dense pattern of settlement long before the industrial revolution gave the process a new purpose. These herring fishers' cottages at Whitby, Yorkshire, were terraced at the beginning of the eighteenth century.

1 John Morley *Life of Richard Cobden* T. Fisher Unwin, London 1881

productive powers of society, that the development of the principles of mass housing during the nineteenth century must be seen. The pioneering housing and city projects of Owen, Lever and Cadbury, and the planning theories of Howard and Soria y Mata succeeded in revolutionizing the concept and meaning of housing because the success of *development* had made the world into a sounding board for ideas. At the same time the growth of the attitude of mind which had urged the taking of every census led to a growing *identification* of the needs of both individual and community. Central and local administration increasingly assumed a servicing role and the architectural profession began to see a new future in environmental economics and the design of ways of life for whole communities. The entire century was so occupied with the problem of accommodation in bursting cities and desolate countryside that by 1900 the meaning of the house had become immersed in the meaning of *housing*, a process in which the financing, planning, construction and administration of dwellings was combined into a complex whole.

The Industrial Revolution began in Britain with a sudden and dramatic increase in population. It is now estimated that the 9 million population of 1801 represented an increase of about 50 per cent over that of 1750. By 1811 an increase of a further 14 per cent was recorded, and between then and 1821 the rate of increase rose to over 20 per cent: by 1901 the population of Britain was over 40 million. This increase was further dramatized by massive migrations within the country which caused previously highly populated areas to become less crowded while the wild northern counties, with their coal and iron resources, became centres of population almost overnight. New factories followed new techniques of production and the textile industry alone, which in 1818 had employed 57,000 workers, by 1840 employed half a million[1].

To the positive attractions of the new industrial towns was added the negative pressure of land enclosures. The pursuit of the same ruthless efficiency in agriculture as had revolutionized manufacture brought about the removal of common rights over land and

(6) The Preston cottages condemned by the Royal Commission, 1844. Earth closets in the back yard of each dwelling, often accompanied by pig-sties, discharged into the central drain visible here. The brutal siting of the cottage and the mill in the distance are also worthy of note.

the fencing in and cultivation of previously open grazing. Small farmers and small-holders left for the towns. By this means the process of gradual urbanization which had gone on since town life first began, suddenly assumed cancerous proportions and the traditional reliance of the nation upon agriculture eroded away.

In Britain, as in the European countries which shortly followed her, the new demography created an unprecedented demand for housing in a new and concentrated form, expressing the highly centralized needs of a country as yet without efficient means of public transport. As a result dwellings were built for rental at a phenomenal density and as cheaply as possible. In Britain the form of the housing differed little at first from the traditional farm labourer's cottage, although later on tenements on the continental model made their appearance as part of a general effort to increase the efficiency of land use. The cottages were packed tightly together in long rows with communal earth closets and often only a single water pump per row. Under these congested conditions primitive hygiene and sanitation revealed inadequacies scarcely noticeable before; cesspools overflowed, drainage was either blocked or non-existent and water supply became polluted.

The pursuit of higher densities and cheaper ways of building, besides leading to the construction of tenements (mostly in the older cities), also brought the 'back to back' cottage into prominence. This type of dwelling, in which two separate units shared the same roof, had sometimes been used in rural practice before; now it became commonplace. Like the Mansard roof in the speculative suburban developments of a century later, it found a new lease of life in circumstances far removed from those in which it was conceived. Economic ingenuity reached the stage in Preston in the north of England where rows of cottages were built with earth closets at the rear which discharged into a central open drain. The contents of this drain flowed into a cesspool whence, twice a year, they were sold as manure by the landlord.

(7) A street in Newcastle-upon-Tyne, about 1855.

Extreme abuses of this kind continued until the Reform Bill of 1832 readjusted constituency boundaries so that the new towns could return members to Parliament. Until then many of them had escaped the surveillance of such environmental legislation as was in existence by the simple expedient of being without charters and without political representation: a state of affairs which worked to the advantage of the unscrupulous.

In view of the appalling social conditions which the untrammelled progress of industrialization created, it is important to note that the vast majority of those individuals drawn into industrial work from agriculture did so because it represented a real improvement over their former condition. Freedom from direct servitude, a flexible private economy based on money instead of food, work which was comparatively highly paid and which women and children could also do, all conspired to encourage the poor to leave the land. The accommodation to which they moved was as good as, if not superior to that which they left; it was only in time that overcrowding, a decline in real wages, worsening conditions of work and the spread of disease focused attention on conditions

1 Edwin Chadwick
Sanitary Conditions of the
Labouring Population in
England Aldine 1842

which in rural isolation had gone unnoticed for centuries. It was *population concentration* which made the defects of the old patterns of living suddenly manifest; disease, high infant mortality and short life expectancy had always been the lot of the poor but suddenly an inescapable picture of communal misery (allied to the increasing economic value to the employer of each of his workers) showed that the inhuman use of human beings had reached a point of diminishing returns.

Edwin Chadwick's report on the sanitary

condition of the labouring classes in the London of 1838 stressed a basically *economic* concern for the wellbeing of workers, and this was the motive which carried through most of the early measures of reform. Recalling that 'in general all epidemics and other infectious diseases are attended with charges, immediate and ultimate, on the poor rates . . .' Chadwick suggested that the cost of dealing with these outbreaks was 'so great as to render it a good economy on the part of the administrators of the poor-laws to incur the charges for *preventing the evils*'[1]. To this end he proposed the construction of a general sewage system, increased control over water supplies (which with private companies were frequently turned off when the landlord neglected to pay his rates), wider streets and legislation to control over-crowding.

Spurred on by a fortuitous outbreak of cholera a Board of Health was set up under the noted philanthropist Lord Shaftesbury. Although speedily abolished when confidence returned (*The Times* editorializing boldly 'We prefer to take our chance of

(8, 9) Harassed by public health legislation in the last quarter of the nineteenth century, developers turned to the 'tunnel-backed' house and to other compromises between density and profit. The tunnel backs – so called because of the narrow passage formed between each pair of outhouses at the rear – illustrated here are from Birmingham (8), while the terraced flats with twin-front doors were built in Newcastle (9). These were still in existence by 1938 when the photograph was taken.

(10) The construction of large tenements in the older cities of both Europe and America continued unabated into the twentieth century. Land values and densities here were too high for low-rise cottages and in Britain only the rent controls of World War I made the private construction of such tenements uneconomical. These apartments were built by the Peabody Trust in Holborn, London, and date from the last quarter of the nineteenth century. New York tenements of a similar period show distinct similarities.

1 *Report of the Royal
Commission examining the
condition of the Urban Poor*
London 1887

cholera and the rest than to be bullied into health'), it nevertheless established a level of official interest which from then on steadily increased as it became evident that typhus and cholera were no respecters of social class.

In 1855 all existing British legislation governing dwellings was consolidated under the Nuisances Removal and Diseases Prevention Act. A decade later powers of compulsory purchase and demolition were incorporated in the Artisans' and Labourers' Dwellings Act. Against this rising tide of restrictive legislation the small developers turned to the 'tunnel-backed house' – a terraced two-storey dwelling with an outhouse and small yard at the rear to comply with public health regulations. The larger organizations concentrated on multi-storey tenements built for allegedly philanthropic motives. Of these the most famous were built in London by the Peabody Trust, whose operations brought in a dividend of $3\frac{1}{2}$ per cent. The failure of this organization, and similar ones such as the Waterlow (which paid even higher dividends), to touch the real problem of the urban poor stemmed from the simple fact that however low the philanthropists made the return on their investment, the rents necessary to maintain it were always higher

than the lowest paid worker could afford. As was to happen with local authority housing in the next century, although for administrative rather than financial reasons, the *mechanism* of welfare was impeding its operation. A Royal Commission appointed in 1884 took evidence from the London Trades Council to the following effect: 'it is totally impossible that private enterprise, philanthropy and charity can ever keep pace with the present demands . . . Economic forces and population have outstepped their endeavours; hence evils accrue. But what the individual cannot do the state municipality must seek to accomplish . . . for it alone possesses the necessary power and wealth.'[1] In embryo this was the line of attack adopted by most of the nations of Europe after World War I.

The Garden City

This conclusion was not however the limit of the nineteenth-century reformists' proposals. Clearly imprinted on their minds was the image of the overcrowded industrial city as the root cause of social evils, ranging from plague and crime to immorality and the frittering away of public funds. Numerous efforts had already been made to integrate industry with the pastoral life of the village. Robert Owen had proposed model industrial villages in Scotland as early as 1816, Titus Salt had built Saltaire in the 1850s, George Cadbury built Bournville in 1879 and Owen Lever Port Sunlight in 1888. In Germany Count Rumford had proposed similar designs as early as 1790. But the 'ideal synthesis' between country and town was not stumbled upon until the very end of the century when, incorporating that other great innovation of the nineteenth century, the railway, Ebenezer Howard proposed a Garden City whose financial constitution promised for the first time to exploit the increase in land values (which had hitherto hindered the construction of low-cost housing in towns) for the benefit of the inhabitants.

(11) The appearance of industry in areas rich in raw materials but otherwise unpopulated brought about enormous environmental changes. The industrialization of the Rhondda Valley in Wales illustrates the results.

Howard's ideas, expounded in a book *Tomorrow, a Peaceful Path to Real Reform*, published in 1898, still influence official planning policy in Britain and elsewhere to this day. Eschewing the utopian approach of earlier reformers, Howard's proposals combined a simple purpose – to bring people back to the land – with elementary but sound economic notions of how this was to be achieved. Basing his argument on the demonstrable proposition that agricultural land converted to urban use *automatically increased in value* Howard proposed that garden-city development companies should be formed to purchase sites and lease plots to those wishing to build. The increasing value of the land thus developed would accrue to the company, which would then finance community services and municipally owned buildings. By this means Howard hoped to avoid the charges of corruption and profiteering which seemed at the time to naturally follow upon efforts to combine philanthropy with profit.[1] The community ownership principle was also intended to prevent the exercise of the kind of paternalism which was occasionally found objectionable at Bournville and Port Sunlight.[2]

Within a year of the publication of the book the Garden City Association was formed. In 1902 the industrialists Cadbury and Lever offered sufficient support for a company to be founded and a pioneer site at Letchworth, thirty-four miles from London, was purchased in the following year. Unfortunately an unpredictable consequence of the simple economics of the garden-city project now came to light. Howard had not envisaged the city company offering any financial assistance to those who were to actually *build* apart from the inducements of cheap leases and low rates. All housing was to have been paid for by individuals or co-operatives. As a result the process of growth at Letchworth was agonizingly slow: drainage, water supply, some roads and less than a dozen houses were all that existed by 1905, when Owen Lever, after failing to persuade the board to sell plots direct to developers in order to get things moving, resigned. As a last desperate effort a cheap cottages exhibition was organized on the site of the moribund Garden City and 121 dwellings were built, an expedient which, by a narrow margin, roused enough interest to avoid ignominious failure.

With the doubtful exception of the as yet unproven linear city concept of Soria y Mata (1885), which antedates the publication

1 An account of some contemporary scandals is given by John Nelson Tarn in 'Some Pioneer Suburban Houses Estates' *Architectural Review* May 1968

2 The Secretary of the Bolton branch of the Engineers Union told Lever (then Lord Leverhulme) that 'no man of an independent turn of mind could breathe for long in the atmosphere of Port Sunlight'. Quoted by Basil Honikman in 'Port Sunlight and the Garden City Movement' *Systems, Building and Design* October 1968

(12) Port Sunlight Village.

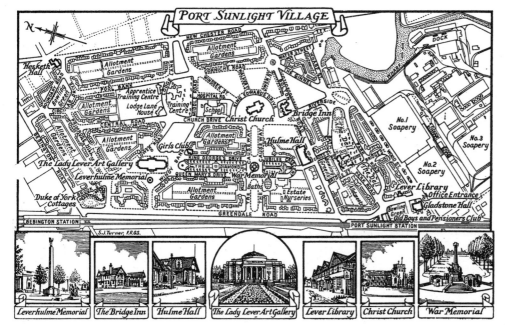

15

1 *Seebohm Committee Report on the Organization and Responsibilities of the Local Authority Personal Social Services in England and Wales* London 1968

of Howard's influential book, the garden-city idea represents the most potent legacy of nineteenth-century environmental thought. Conceived before the mass adoption of private transport, and indifferent to the style of dwelling used within it, the garden-city idea has demonstrated remarkable resilience. In Britain Letchworth was joined in 1919 by Welwyn, and then in 1946 by the first generation of publicly financed New Towns. All over Europe and America the bowdlerized form of garden city, generally called garden suburb, proliferated steadily after 1904. Many were built before the Great War in Sweden, France and Germany, including a fine example at Essen named after Baroness Bertha Krupp von Bohlen, who later christened the enormous artillery pieces which shelled Paris from a range of seventy miles.

However, the growth of organized housing also took a more bureaucratic form. Between the passing of the British Housing of the Working Classes Act of 1890 and the outbreak of war a considerable body of housing and planning legislation was passed all over Europe. At the same time the foundations for direct government involvement in the process of housing were laid by the growth of government involvement in all spheres of welfare. Social security and national insurance acts were passed, trades unions achieved recognized status, unemployment benefits were begun and free education, minimum wage rates and controlled conditions of work became commonplace. The increasingly socialized legislation of Europe naturally embraced the concepts of planning and the provision of housing for reasons which still seemed compelling seventy years later when the Seebohm Report[1] to the British government noted that 'in our society the maintenance of family life and the care and upbringing of children are dependent upon the possession of an adequate home. Family and housing are inextricably linked. Loss of

(13) An original Ebenezer Howard diagram from *Tomorrow, a peaceful path to real reform*, published in 1898. The principles of economic autarky and anti-urbanism implicit in all Garden City projects can be clearly identified here – together with the notion of a finite population.

(14) Letchworth Garden City from the air. The radial concept idealized in Howard's diagrams is still present at Letchworth (begun 1903) but sixteen years later developed into a grid-iron at Welwyn (15). The orbital railway which figured in Howard's theories was tried out at Welwyn but later abandoned. In both cases the relationship of the town centre to the mainline railway is exactly as Howard suggested.

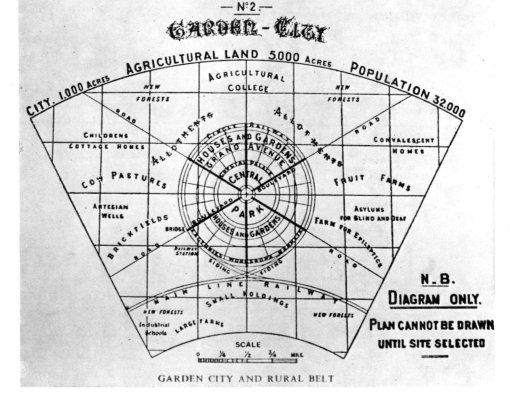

GARDEN CITY AND RURAL BELT

16

(15) Welwyn Garden City.

or failure to acquire a secure and decent home places a family in jeopardy.'

Generally public-health oriented in the latter years of the nineteenth century, most European housing legislation was concerned with either the provision of adequate finance for the continued construction of low-cost dwellings – which was no longer profitable – or the establishment of legislative machinery able to condemn unfit property and control new development. In Belgium an act of 1889 made government funds available at low-interest rates to finance the construction of dwellings for industrial employees. In 1894 similar measures were enacted in France leading to the establishment in 1912 of the *Office Publique d'Habitations à Bon Marché*, an organization of regional public authorities empowered to loan funds for house building as well as subsidize needy tenants or purchasers. An Italian law of 1908 also authorized low-interest loans to co-operative societies. During the same period much primary planning legislation was passed. A Dutch act of 1901 not only required every community with a population of over 10,000 to prepare development plans incorporating specific proposals for new housing, but also provided for the public-authority construction of dwellings as well as the usual low-interest loans to co-operatives. More extreme measures were adopted in Germany where (as elsewhere) overcrowding in cities and spiralling land values had made property manipulation a major scandal. In Frankfurt indignation was so strong that in 1902 the Mayor was able to enact an ordinance pooling slum property, redesignating its use in accordance with a city development plan, and redistributing it leasehold for redevelopment. Up to 40 per cent of the land thus seized was to be retained without compensation for streets, parks and other municipal uses. This *Lex Adickes*, one of the most extreme pieces of planning legislation enacted before 1919, was to prove an incalculable benefit to the housing activities of the post-war administration of Frankfurt. In Britain the Housing and Town Planning Act of 1909 echoed the main provisions of the Dutch act of 1901 with additional powers to encourage the preservation of rural areas and important buildings, and bring about concerted action by neighbouring administrations over wider areas.

Despite this widespread politicization of the problem there is little doubt that without the consummate disaster of World War I, neither the patient enthusiasm of the garden-city advocates, nor the determination of reforming legislators, would have wrought the immense changes in the genesis of mass housing that the first quarter of the twentieth century in fact saw. The legislation passed during the period of reform which succeeded the cholera terrors of the urban/industrial concentrations of the mid-nineteenth century was in many cases only nominal in its effect. In Britain, the act of 1890 and its successors were all but failures in terms of dwellings completed as a public service. In the twenty-three years before 1913 the total number of tenements, lodging houses and houses built by local authorities was a mere 14,000 – an average of 600 dwellings per year. Rural demolitions brought the net figure down to a bare 8000 dwellings, all built by the tiny percentage of local authorities who took any action at all under the provisions of the housing acts. 99 per cent of all dwellings completed between 1890 and 1910 were the products of private enterprise. In Britain the weekly rental of accommodation built to the reigning standards of market profitability was the lot of the overwhelming mass of the people – a situation which also obtained in other European countries.

20

2 The birth of the public sector

'. . . it is totally impossible that private enterprise, philanthropy and charity can ever keep pace with the present demands . . . Economic forces and population have outstepped their endeavours; hence evils accrue. But what the individual cannot do the State municipality must seek to accomplish . . . for it alone possesses the necessary power and wealth.'

Evidence given by the London Trades Council to the Royal Commission examining the condition of the urban poor, 1887.

World War I changed the housing situation dramatically and permanently. Within months of its outbreak credit restrictions, financial uncertainty, requisitioning, shortage of materials and the growing demands of total war brought house building to a standstill in all the belligerent nations. Obeying the economic rules of the free market the price of houses and, more significantly, the rents charged by landlords rose steeply. Grave hardship was postponed by the expedient of government rent control, introduced in Britain by the Rent Restriction Act of 1915 and in France and Germany later in the war, by which time rents in the latter country had increased, on an average, to four times their pre-war value. In Russia one of the first decrees of the Bolsheviks after their accession to power in October 1917 nationalized all urban housing and handed it over to municipal Soviets for redistribution to the poorest people. Two months later this measure was succeeded by a further decree banning all private real-estate transactions, sales, leases and mortgages.[1] As a result the former occupants of spacious apartments were crammed into one room and the flood of immigrants into all urban areas increased; a situation which accorded perfectly with the advice contained in the bold text of Engels which Lenin allegedly read and annotated immediately before the revolution.[2] Engels maintained that it was sheer utopianism to work out the details of housing allocation before

the revolution – all that was necessary was the certainty that sufficient accommodation existed in physical form. From that point on 'rational utilization' could always be achieved by 'expropriation of the present owners and by quartering in their houses the homeless or those workers excessively crowded in their former dwellings'.[3] This simple and ruthless policy was, like the expedient of rent restriction in less drastically disturbed countries, temporarily effective. It served its purpose throughout the period of the intervention and the civil war. That flat- and house-sharing might still be commonplace in Soviet Russia forty years later was a thought which crossed no one's mind – save that of the dispossessed *bourgeois* himself.

Milder though they might have been than Russian nationalization, the wartime rent restriction laws of the other European nations none the less presaged a more serious phase of government intervention in the previously free housing market. For the first time the traditional pattern of enterprise was blocked by a deliberate restriction on the yield of projects whose cost could not be similarly held down. In Britain this simple procedure, which continued for most of the next forty years, practically extinguished the private landlord as a housing entrepreneur. At the same time, although it did not make postwar government-subsidized housing *inevitable*, rent restriction sacrificed long-term

(16) Part of the development of 20,000 tenement dwellings built at great profit on the site of the former fortifications of the city of Paris. Intended originally as a major slum clearance project embracing the crowded tenements penned in by the fortifications, the whole operation was appallingly mishandled and the resulting buildings merely worsened overcrowding in the areas concerned. Le Corbusier's 'Îlôt Insalubre' project of 1936 was a response to the scandal created by the completion of the scheme.

1 Berthold Lubetkin 'Town and Landscape Planning in Soviet Russia' *The Architectural Association Journal* January 1933

2 D. V. Donnison '*The Government of Housing*' Penguin Books, London 1967

3 This quotation, taken from Donnison *op. cit.* is from Frederick Engels *The Housing Question* Lawrence Wishart, London 1936

market stability for short-term relief. Its effect in all countries where it was applied, exaggerated by the unexpectedly disastrous course of the war itself, was to ensure government involvement in an *inevitable* post-war housing crisis.

The possible dimensions of this crisis became clearer in 1917 when accumulating evidence began to indicate that inadequate housing was likely to cost far more in social terms than financial. In Britain alone conscription had thrown into sharp relief the fact that an alarmingly large number of recruits rejected on medical grounds came from depressed urban areas. Efforts to increase war production had revealed that 4 million working weeks per year were being lost through sickness attributable to bad environmental conditions. Medical examination of 2·5 million schoolchildren indicated that nearly two-thirds were physically defective, and a Royal Commission appointed to look into the causes of industrial unrest reported that lack of adequate housing accommodation was the most common cause of discontent among workers. Finally another Royal Commission sitting in Scotland disclosed that more than

half the population lived in houses of one or two rooms, while one-fifth of all Scottish families lived in one room only. In Britain as a whole it was estimated that 500,000 new houses would be needed to compensate for the arrested building of the preceding three years.

Revelations such as these combined uneasily with growing evidence that Europe was bankrupting herself in the prosecution of a stalemate war. One by one the governments and constitutions of the combatant states faced collapse or near collapse. Massive mutinies almost caused the defeat of the French army in 1917; in the same year Czarist rule in Russia came to an end and revolutionary fervour swept Europe. Germany herself collapsed into temporary anarchy in the autumn of 1918 and the war ended with the Balkanization of the two great European powers of Germany and Austria-Hungary. Between August 1914 and November 1918 destruction of life, property and institutions occurred on a scale unmatched since medieval times: the losses sustained by the major powers from action and disease have been variously estimated at between 11 and 12

(17) Loucheur housing, so called after the Loucheur Act of 1928, was generally centred around Paris and did little to improve housing conditions throughout the rest of France. The development illustrated here shows Place Principale, Cité-Jardin Cashan. Architect: Louis Feine 1929.

million persons, and a further 8 million died in the influenza epidemic which closely followed the end of hostilities. The number of births prevented by these casualties was probably in the region of a further 10 million. It is against such a background that the dramatically different post-war attitude to housing must be seen: Europe was miraculously to be given a second chance.

Perversely, in the United States the war had stimulated Federal housing action for the first time. The large housing requirements generated by the industrial expansion needed to cope with war production called into being two new agencies: the Housing Division of the Emergency Fleet Corporation, and the United States Housing Corporation (USHC). Of these the former completed a small number of dwellings by the end of the war (9000 family units and 7500 single-person units), while the latter failed to complete any of its 25,000 projected dwellings until after the Armistice, when some 6000 family units were sold off according to the terms of wartime construction. Closely resembling British garden suburbs, these developments represented the only housing

construction of any importance achieved by combatants during World War I. Despite this promising performance Federal interest in housing evaporated after 1918 and although many interesting developments were completed in the private sector, including Radburn (the original vehicle-segregated, low-density layout), it was not until the Wall Street Crash of 1929, massive mortgage foreclosures, and Roosevelt's 'New Deal' that Federal housing activity was resumed.

Of the major European nations only France and Britain combined acute need with the political and economic stability and enthusiasm necessary to embark on a massive housing drive. In France the opportunity was not seized: near bankruptcy, war damage and the crippling loss of 1·5 million men had gravely weakened her resources. Ambitious plans to rebuild the congested slums which in the nineteenth century had grown up around the ring of fortifications enclosing the city of Paris, disintegrated into scandalous profiteering when the cleared sites of the fortresses were leased at the height of the depression to private developers for the construction of 20,000 sub-standard tenement dwellings in closely packed eight-storey blocks – leaving the neighbouring slums intact. The Loucheur Act itself, the major housing act of the post-war period which provided for the adequate financing of low-cost dwellings, was only passed in 1928 after five years of lobbying. Authorizing the immediate construction of 500,000 dwellings and taking over and amplifying the work of the pre-war *Office Public*, it nevertheless failed to reverse the process of concentration upon the Paris area that the *Office* had indirectly encouraged by its emphasis upon piecemeal suburban housing. Until the Popular Front government of the late 1930s French housing administration wallowed in a morass of regional demoralization and incompetence.

In Britain this situation tended to occur in reverse. Enormous energy and idealism were liberated in the immediate post-war period by the emphasis the 1918 Lloyd George government placed on a 'Land fit for heroes to live in' and 'Homes for heroes', while the late '30s saw a growing demoralization

1 *Tudor-Walters
Committee Report* London
1918

2 *Tudor-Walters
Committee Report* London
1918

resulting from the comparative failure of what was to have been a definitive slum clearance programme. In 1919, however, there was no indication that the housing problem would resist solution by drastic action. Recognizing that because of inflation and the chronic shortage of skilled labour (which was to persist for some time as all apprenticeship schemes had broken down during the war) housing could not now be provided profit-

in Britain despite the rapid development of large towns and urban centres, and the consequent 'freedom from tenement dwellings' characteristic of the British Isles 'had been regarded with envy by those countries and cities which have had the misfortune to adopt the tenement system to any great extent'.[2] Wholesale adoption of this design principle by local authorities, coupled with its notorious popularity in the private sector,

ably at rents people could afford, the newly formed Ministry of Health – which was to retain control of housing until 1951 – decided to open the entrepreneurial coffers of the local authorities by undertaking to bear any costs incurred beyond a certain specified amount on every house which the authorities erected. The Addison Act of 1919 which put these proposals into effect marked the arrival of housing as a major item of government expenditure – a position which it has not since relinquished.

The Addison Act seized upon a report, published in the previous year under the chairmanship of Sir John Tudor-Walters, on 'questions of building construction in connection with the provision of dwellings for the working classes in England and Wales and Scotland and . . . upon methods of securing economy and despatch in the provision of such dwellings'.[1] The fourth section of this report dealt with the type of accommodation required by the 'working classes' and discussed alternative designs, of which the most suitable was deemed to be the 'self-contained cottage'. This type of dwelling, the report pointed out, had continued to be the customary means of housing

ensured that the vast majority of the 4 million dwellings completed before 1939 were of this configuration. Even contemporary British experiments in prefabrication were confined to the 'self-contained cottage' image. As a result modern architecture tended to be confined to that tiny sector of the private market financed by wealthy enthusiasts; and a potential conflict of styles within the public sector between the exponents of the 'values' of traditional housing and the advocates of 'revolutionary functionalism', was defused. Largely as a result of Tudor-Walters, the defence of modern design in Britain between the wars involved little more than pouring scorn on the inhabitants of mock-Tudor mansions by inviting them to wear doublet and hose to the office:[1] in Germany (as we shall see) it became a matter of professional life or death.

1 This taunt seemed to please many modernists: both F. R. S. Yorke *The Modern House* Architectural Press 1934, and Anthony Bertram *Design* Penguin Books 1938, repeat it.

(18 & 19) Two aspects of the 'self-contained cottage' image enshrined in the Tudor-Walters report of 1918. The local-authority estate (18) at Allens Cross, Birmingham, was completed in 1928 and contrasts strongly with the attempts to provide working-class housing illustrated in chapter one. There is also a subtle but clear distinction between it and the contemporaneous estate of semi-detached privately owned houses at Watford (19).

1   Gilbert and Elizabeth
Glen McAllister *Town and
Country Planning* Faber
and Faber, London 1941

Critics of the Addison Act, with its open-ended government commitment, anticipated great difficulties and these were not slow in arriving. Unused as they were to the exercise of their new powers many local authorities demonstrated both stupidity and negligence in their administration of housing programmes. In Liverpool contracts to the value of £2 million were placed with a firm which, having a paid up capital of only £3000 subsequently went bankrupt and left the authority and the government to face an enormous loss. Rising building costs were simply passed on to the government with the result that the cost of the Addison Act to the taxpayer in terms of local-authority subsidies amounted to almost £1 per week for every house built.[1] Under a rising barrage of criticism Addison resigned and the government limited the number of houses to be built under the terms of the 1919 Act to 176,000. Clearly, under these conditions, there could be no question of repealing the Rent Restriction Act: it was consolidated in 1920 and renewed with minor modifications throughout the inter-war period.

Addison's grandiloquent foray into publicly subsidized housing was succeeded in the wintry economic climate of 1923 by a new Conservative plan, the excessively modest Chamberlain Act, which offered a low government subsidy to local authorities, conditional financial aid to private builders, and local-authority mortgages for those with sufficient savings to purchase their own dwellings. Under this law 438,047 houses were completed by the outbreak of World War II. A third major housing act (the Wheatley Act) was passed in 1924 under Britain's first socialist administration. This Act, drafted in consultation with representatives of the building industry, laid down that the latter were to carry through at least two-thirds of a 2·5 million unit housing programme within fifteen years in return for increased subsidies to the local authorities. The number of houses necessary was computed on the basis of an annual rate of 100,000 for the fifteen years, plus a million houses to make good the deficiencies brought about by the war. In terms of performance this act was the most successful of the inter-war period, producing 520,298 houses

at a cost of only £41 million by March 1939.

This early period of widespread activity in Britain had not been emulated on the continent. In Russia the end of the civil war and the expulsion of interventionist troops left industrial production at a low ebb, urban facilities and services reduced to one-fifth of their pre-war capacity, and a crucial shortage of technicians and skilled labour. All building maintenance had ceased and the population – savagely depleted by starvation and disease – was crowded into half-ruined cities in search of work which scarcely existed. Under these conditions dwellings had to be provided at all costs and under the New Economic Policy the Draconian acts of 1917 were partially repealed. Houses were returned to their former owners in return for guaranteed repairs, and taxation relief was arranged in order to stimulate private initiative. Individuals were given free land provided they agreed to build houses, on leases of sixty-five years if construction was in stone, and fifty years if in timber. The right of inheritance and sale was temporarily restored. Finally a special decree of December 1926 offered complete freedom of land use for collective dwellings. This situation led to the arrival in the USSR of many European architects and engineers, and encouraged some American and German sources to finance building there.

In 1927 the first Soviet decree covering rents set figures as a proportion of current wage levels. Although relatively high by contemporary European standards these figures were to remain maxima for the next twenty-five years.

Germany, next to Russia, was the country whose economy and social structure was most drastically altered by the war. In both cases the traditional pyramid of power collapsed, and though in Germany the adroit action of certain bankers and militarists maintained the semblance of continuous central government, in practice industrial and civil unrest, currency crises, the loss of a major industrial area (the Ruhr), several attempted coups and the steady impoverishment and alienation of the middle classes through the erosion of their capital, main-

(20) A Soviet Collective in Moscow, designed by M. Y. Ginsburg and completed in 1929. Designed to serve 200 people with many communal facilities the building is a curious forerunner of the enormous *Unités d'habitation* of Le Corbusier, as well as of a a style of urban low-cost housing which enjoyed a considerable vogue in urban Britain during the 1960s.

tained the revolutionary situation which had ended the war. In such conditions (as in Russia) the rhetoric of designers, artists and unemployed ex-soldiers corresponded closely to reality. To read the violent post-war effusions of the architects Taut, Scharoun, Luckhardt, Behne, and Gropius today without reference to the disintegrated state of their world is to fail to understand the nihilistic genesis of the famous Weimar housing effort. In Germany to advocate the construction of dwellings and other buildings in steel and glass implied a simultaneous rejection of the traditions of that Imperial Germany which had visited such ruin and disgrace upon its people, trampling on a sea of discarded uniforms and psychoses with eyes fixed upon the crystal-hard image of an architecture uncontaminated by formal echoes of that catastrophic era. Gropius wrote in 1919: 'the old forms are in ruins, the benumbed world is shaken up, the old human spirit is invalidated and in flux toward a new form'.[1] While Taut editorialized in the first issue of his short-lived magazine *Dawn*: 'our (traditional) concepts, "space", "homeland", "style"! To hell with them, odious concepts! Destroy them, break them up! Nothing shall remain! Break up your academies, spew out the old fogies . . . Blast! Blast! Let our North wind blow through this musty, threadbare, tattered world.'[2] In the programme of the *Arbeitsrat fur Kunst* of December 1918 he demanded enormous experimental grounds for the testing of glass and steel buildings for the inspection and approval of the people, the cost to be borne by the sale of 'material melted down from monuments, from dismantled triumphal avenues and so on'.[3] Neither Gropius nor Taut were mere propagandists: the former's tenure of office at the *Bauhaus* was but a prelude to an illustrious international career, while Taut was appointed Director of Municipal Construction at Magdeburg in 1921 and later became chief designer for *Gehag*, the enormous Berlin housing co-operative, supervising some of

1 Barbara Miller Lane *Architecture and Politics in Germany 1918–1945* Harvard University Press, Cambridge Massachusetts 1968

2 Barbara Miller Lane *Architecture and Politics in Germany 1918–1945* Harvard University Press, Cambridge Massachusetts 1968

3 Ulrich Conrads and Hans Sperlich *Fantastic Architecture* Architectural Press, London 1963

the most important housing developments of the Weimar era. The fact that men of such radical and intemperate views rose to positions of considerable administrative power all over Germany shows clearly the gulf that separated German from British, or even French experience at the time. Le Corbusier's utterances of the same period were as violent, if less desperate: but there was never any question of the French government implementing his 'Citrohan' programme.

The first intimations of what was afoot came from Gropius's newly formed Bauhaus in 1922 when exhibitions of housing layouts and designs for a tract of land promised to the school by the Social Democratic government of Saxe-Weimar were given in Weimar and Berlin. Although little came of this project the exhibitions were influential both as images of the new form of housing, and as harbingers of what economic advantages might be expected from modular design and prefabrication.

Like Le Corbusier, Gropius had long advocated mass production and design rationalization as the key to the housing problem, and with the stabilization of the mark in 1924 the opportunity arrived. By far the strongest force available for the major housing effort Germany needed was the co-operative housing movement – composed of organizations representing all the major trades and professions – which had sprung into being during the last decade of the nineteenth century to combat the profiteering of private landlords. The position of these societies had been greatly strengthened by rigid rent control and when in 1924 a special Federal rent tax (*Hauszinsteuer*) was imposed on that proportion of rent above pre-war level, the large sums of money that became available were distributed between the 4300 societies, and the limited dividend development companies which formed the second arm of the Weimar housing effort. Both types of organization were supervised by municipal authorities, but the urgency and economy which characterized the programme effectively prevented any aesthetic censorship in those cities where determined urban authorities employed radical architects, or the architects

themselves were able to control planning, loans, design and the administration of building regulations – a situation which occurred in Frankfurt after 1924 and some years later in Berlin.

In Frankfurt, Ernst May, a protegé of Mayor Landmann, the planning enthusiast and inheritor of the not inconsiderable powers of the *Lex Adickes*, was appointed Director of Municipal Construction. May had worked for a time with Raymond Unwin in England and was a confirmed 'garden city' advocate; he and Landmann agreed that slum clearance and redevelopment should be subordinated to the construction of a series of satellite suburbs ringing the city at a distance of about five miles from its centre. Only a part of this programme was completed by 1933 but the most impressive section, a line of adjoining suburbs to the north-west, Praunheim, Romerstadt and Westhausen, was finished by 1930 and clearly revealed the image May had cast for 'Das Neue Frankfurt'. In complete opposition to the 'self-contained cottage' pattern of contemporary British public housing, May's terraced two- and three-storeyed houses and apartments featured roof-top drying facilities, central heating and a degree of open planning to compensate for the exceptionally small floor

(21) Praunheim, Romerstadt and Westhausen seen from across the Nidda valley to the north-west of the Frankfurt of the late 1920s. Built using Ernst May's *Massivblock* system of prefabrication – which was later employed for many years in derivative forms in the USSR – 'Das Neue Frankfurt' was one of the triumphs of the Weimar modernists and exerted enormous influence on later architectural attitudes to mass housing.

space allocated to each person.[1] Schools, shops, guest houses, churches and a theatre were either provided or planned and large areas of open space were included, although houses, gardens and allotments were not always contiguous. Extensive use was made of a pre-cast concrete prefabrication system known as *massivblock*.

In Berlin the initial impetus for a similar kind of housing did not come from the city administration but one of the Berlin building societies, the *Gemeinnützige Heimstätten Aktiengesellschaft*, or *Gehag*, which had been formed by the merging of several smaller societies in 1924. Under the leadership of Martin Wagner, an official of the Berlin-Schöneberg building department, *Gehag* secured the services of Bruno Taut as its chief architect and embarked on the

1 Goering described these houses as 'stalls for animals'

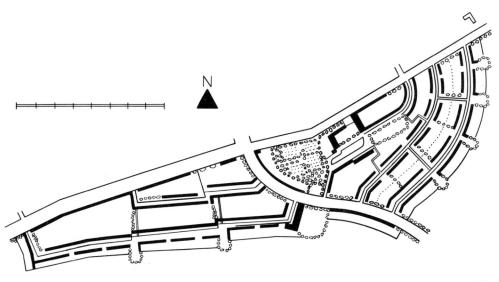

N

(22) A block plan of the suburb of Romerstadt showing the extended curves of the terraced houses and apartment buildings with communal gardens. This pattern of public-sector development was widely imitated as late as the 1960s.

(23) The Hufeisensiedlung Berlin-Britz. Contemporaneous with May's work at Frankfurt, Taut and Wagner's work around Berlin was generally built to a higher density, reflecting the higher land values of the German capital.

construction of a number of large garden suburbs on the outskirts of Berlin, each one comprising several thousand dwellings. Higher land prices necessitated higher densities than at Frankfurt so the 'horseshoe suburb, (Hufeisensiedlung) at Berlin-Britz, and the 'forest suburb' (Waldsiedlung) at Berlin-Zehlendorf, consisted almost entirely of three-storey apartment buildings with communal lawns and gardens between, and slightly larger floor areas than at Frankfurt. Like May, Wagner and Taut experimented with prefabrication techniques, but they also employed building guild labour (as did some local authorities in Britain during the life of the Addison Act) to reduce costs.

Probably the most famous of the Berlin housing developments was Siemensstadt, a large suburb comprising long three- and four-storey apartment blocks financed by the Siemens group employees' building society which had been established in 1914. Begun in 1929 the project was shared between Gropius, Scharoun, Häring, Forbat, Bartning and Hertlein, all well-known radical architects; the result, with district heating, school, shops and church was one of the definitive achievements of the Weimar housing programme.

On the planning front the major breakthrough was the rapid discovery of entirely new concepts of layout and orientation, which began with the exploration of new arrangements of three- or four-storey buildings around the periphery of the traditional housing block. This freed the central space for recreation and service areas and was widely used in Hamburg suburbs such as Possmorweg, completed in 1928. Later the increasing use of virgin sites freed designers from the grid-iron implications of the urban block and long terraces of housing and flats began to line residential service roads, with through traffic skirting the perimeter of the site as at Praunheim and Romerstadt. Further study of planning problems led to a greater emphasis on orientation. East-west exposure became mandatory and efforts to obtain it led to a final dislocation of the traditional relationship between house and

(24) The Weissenhof Siedlung, Stuttgart, built as the second exhibition of the *Deutsche Werkbund* in the form of a modern model suburb. The entire project – which was under the direction of Mies van der Rohe – was a *tour de force* of modern architecture with houses and apartments by most of the European pioneers including Le Corbusier, Oud, Gropius, Scharoun, Mart Stam, Hilberseimer and Taut. Badly damaged during World War II the development has been restored by the German Federal Government since 1955.

street. In the later schemes of the Weimar period (such as Spandau Haselhorst near Berlin), uniform orientation was often achieved over the whole site, with long blocks of dwellings set at right angles to access roads and the space between given over to gardens and pedestrian approaches. Owing to the sudden termination of the Weimar modern phase, these and other revolutionary developments were never subjected to critical evaluation on the basis of user response. It was not until the high-rise crises of the early '60s that anything other than uncritical admiration was directed towards the planning of human settlements on the basis of orientation, economy and (as at Frankfurt) the movement of assembly cranes.

Sedulously publicized and widely admired as were the housing activities of the Weimar pioneers, their output amounted to only a very small proportion of the total housing effort of the republic. May's entire Frankfurt programme comprised only 15,000 dwellings, while the *Gehag* in Berlin built just over 10,000 units between 1924 and 1933. Some of the most famous developments, like the influential Weissenhof Siedlung at Stuttgart – at one time visited by 20,000 people a day – were scarcely serious contributions to the housing problem themselves and represented a sophisticated use of resources intended to help develop more economical means of building.[1] The spread of modern building after 1927 to cities like Magdeburg, Cologne, Breslau, Hamburg and Düsseldorf was seriously impeded by the Depression, while the design ethos of its practitioners came into increasing conflict with emergent Nazi ideas after 1930.

Three of the larger and more traditional building societies operating in the Berlin area, the *Dewog, Gagfah* and *Heimat,* built

(25) Le Corbusier's projected 'Ville Radieuse' of 1930. Unlike the German modernists the great French architect had no opportunity to experiment on any scale before the 1939-45 war. This project, the culmination of three separate earlier efforts to design a complete *ville contemporaine* should be compared to British achievements (14, 15) as well as to Weimar realities in order to sense the variation in thought on urbanism during the inter-war period.

71,000 dwellings in the form of tenements, semi-detached and detached houses between 1924 and 1929 – a performance unequalled by any of the moderns. The total number of dwellings completed between 1918 and 1933 reached 3 million.

In considering the collapse of this immense effort, modern and traditional alike, it is important not to attribute too much importance to the coming of the Nazis, who apart from their conflicting design styles, had as great an interest in maintaining housing output as their predecessors: a fact which is indicated by the considerable growth of the *Gehag* after its takeover in 1932 by the nationalized trades union, the *Deutsch Arbeits Front.* The real cause of the breakdown in Germany as elsewhere was the Depression.

1 According to Miller Lane the money used to construct the Weissenhof Siedlung came from the *Reichsforschungsgesellschaft fur Wirtschaftlichkeit im Bau – und Wohnungswesen* (RFG), founded in 1927 with an appropriation of 10 million RM. This organization was intended to support research into more economical means of building. In practice most of its funds were absorbed by prestige modern projects such as Weissenhof and Dessau.

(26) The Siedlung Herneswiese, part of an enormous complex of high-density working-class suburbs built on the outskirts of Vienna during the pre-Depression period. During the disturbances before the *Anschluss* these buildings, strongholds of the Austrian Communist party, were shelled by the army.

3 The Depression and after

'Vigorous national development alone holds out the prospect of reducing unemployment. Anything short of national measures implies a mere tinkering with the greatest of the evils of the existing economic system. The cry from the distressed areas of "work or maintenance" must be heard now if it is to be heard at all. To provide neither the one nor the other when the means to do so are at our disposal is to be guilty of the worst of national crimes.'

Everybody's Book of Politics London 1938

Europe

Between 1918 and 1933 unemployment figures in Germany only dropped below a million once (in 1927) and thereafter climbed to a peak of over 5 million in 1931. Turnover in the construction industry fell from 9000 million marks in 1929 to just over 4000 million in 1931 – a disaster which alone accounted for one-fifth of the unemployed in the latter year.[1] With capital interest rates still above 8 per cent despite the depression the *Hauszinsteuer* was no longer an effective source of building capital and, in any case, with the breakdown of public-service industries housing was no longer the central problem.

In 1930 Ernst May, with several of his staff, accepted an offer from Moscow to plan new cities in Siberia. Two years later he was joined by Taut. The seizure of state and federal power in 1933 by the Nazis heralded a purge of the most radical staff in schools (including the Bauhaus under Mies van der Rohe), municipal building administrations and building societies. Wagner was summarily dismissed and he and Gropius (who for a time endeavoured to reach an understanding with Goebbels' new Ministry of Propaganda) left with many others for England and America.

Whatever the Weimar diaspora may have expected to find in the outside world there can be little doubt that they were both surprised and disappointed – at least at first. Austria – a brief stopping place for some on the way to the USSR – was undergoing the same political drift as Germany. Of the countries most damaged by the war she had suffered uniquely, being reduced after the armistice from an enormous empire to a small state, about the size of Ireland, with a population of under 8 million, more than a quarter of whom lived in Vienna. Here much tenement housing had been built during the latter part of the nineteenth century and this dwelling type was developed after 1920, despite a registered public preference of two to one for houses. During the entire inter-war period the Vienna public authorities constructed 23,000 apartment units and only 2000 houses, most financed by a *Hauszinsteuer* as in Germany. These buildings achieved some notoriety as a result of their being shelled by the Fascists during the takeover of 1934.

In Russia itself May and Taut must have been appalled at the conditions which greeted them. Struggling to industrialize and electrify one of the most backward nations in Europe, the Bolsheviks had encountered a housing problem without precedent in the western world. Despite rapidly increasing state expenditure (1000 million roubles were

1 *International Unemployment: a study of fluctuations in employment and unemployment in several countries 1910–1930* International Industrial Relations Institute (IRI), The Hague 1932

35

(27) Magnitogorsk at the time of May's arrival in the USSR in 1930. The extent of the task awaiting the architects of the Russian Revolution can be sensed from this original photograph.

(28) The 'Cité de la Muette', Vieux Drancy, by Marcel Lods, built on the outskirts of Paris in the early '30s.

spent on housing in 1931 – as much as the entire expenditure on *all building* in 1928) available floor space per person had decreased from 5·7 square metres in 1928 to 4·4 square metres in 1932 under the pressure of population increase. In the new industrial regions such as Kusbass, the Donetz basin, Magnitogorsk (where May began planning a new manufacturing city) and Kusnetzk (where a population of 70,000 was served by four bath houses) floor space per person had dropped still more to an unbelievable 2·4 square metres. Plans for Garden Cities, linear towns and ideal dwellings coexisted with unimaginable squalor and the threat of complete collapse. In 1931 a new organization for the implementation of standard house construction (*Standargilstroi*) was formed and began the mass production of two basic types of dwelling: a timber, three-storey, felt-roofed house for five to ten families, to be prefabricated at lumber camps; and a five-storey brick tenement block for single persons with lavatories for every two flats, kitchens for every twelve and no baths, to be site built with standard service components in every major city and town.[1]

Such was the reality which greeted the designers of the centrally heated paradises of Romerstadt and Hufeisen.

Of those who drifted west, few stayed in France, where, despite an almost unanimous resolution in favour of low-density, horizontal development taken at the *Quinzaine Internationale d' Urbanisme* held in Paris in 1937, renewed interest was shown in large-scale skyscraper projects of the kind advocated by Le Corbusier more than a decade before. The Department of the Seine planned a series of *cité jardins* of this type to be built on the outskirts of Paris. One, at Drancy, 'La Cité de la Muette',[2] was completed some time before the war only to remain vacant because no transport arrangements had been made to deal with the daily journeys of its inhabitants to work. Much photographed at the time it was requisitioned by the French army in 1939 for use as a barracks. Two other *cité jardins*, 'Chatenay Malabry' (intended to house 20,000 people), and 'Plessis Robinson' were partly occupied by the outbreak of war but public transport was not integrated here either.

1 These facts are taken from 'Town and Landscape Planning in Soviet Russia' an address given by Berthold Lubetkin to the British Institute of Landscape Architects in December 1932 at the Architectural Association in London, *Architectural Association Journal* January 1933

2 The 'La Muette' towers employed a system of pre-cast concrete panels hung on to a steel frame. Invented by the engineer Eugène Mopin this system was applied in modified form at Quarry Hill, Leeds in 1938 with indifferent success.

1 *International Unemployment: a study of fluctuations in employment in several countries 1910–1930* International Industrial Relations Institute (IRI), The Hague 1932.

2 G. and E. G. McAllister *Town and Country Planning* Faber and Faber, London 1941

For most another brief stopping place, this time on the way to the USA, Britain presented a very different but in some ways no more encouraging picture. The striking government intervention of 1919 had not proved as conclusive as many had hoped and although over a million local authority dwellings were to be completed by 1939, the national census of 1931 and the administrative surveys which preceded the 1935 Housing Act indicated that the continuing disparity between the cost of subsidized housing and the rents most prospective tenants could afford to pay, was at best deferring a general solution to the problems of homelessness and overcrowding.

As in Germany post-war housing efforts had been dogged by the repercussions of economic decline. Unemployment averaged over 12 per cent[1] between 1921 and 1930 and rose to over 20 per cent in 1931: world trade slumped, balance of payments problems generated by the First World War remained unsolved and the housing acts, starved of adequate finance, never realized their potential. More economical methods of contracting such as those practised by the building guilds, who operated at cost without fixed tenders and sometimes achieved savings of up to 20 per cent of the cost of individual units, were forced out of existence by the collapse of the Addison Act. Experiments in prefabrication (which will be discussed later) failed to produce significant savings.

An act passed in 1931 to combat the shortage of farm labour by financing the construction of 40,000 rural dwellings, failed almost entirely because a clause designed to expedite the work by demanding loan applications before a specified date was neutralized by a simultaneous appeal for 'economies' until after the date had passed. In the same year the emergency 'National' government attempted a partial reversion to nineteenth-century practice by diverting the local authorities from new building to slum clearance, while guaranteeing to make good the losses incurred in the financing of new building by private-sector mortgages taken out at a higher rate of interest.

Conspicuously unsuccessful as the latter part of this plan was, it has frequently been put forward, since World War II, as a possible means of drawing private-sector money into public-sector construction, and bears a close resemblance to the highly successful Federal Housing Association (FHA) loan procedure established in the USA in 1934. Meanwhile the slum clearance programme itself suffered not a little from a confusion of data. The precise number of unfit dwellings in the country was never agreed: local-authority surveys in 1931 suggested a figure of 300,000; the Council for Research on House Construction found 50,000 more, and the Liberal party claimed that 4 million dwellings would need to be razed or modernized if the programme were to be really successful. Since it was intended that all slums should be cleared by 1938 all these targets were impractical. In the event about 200,000 dwellings were demolished by 1939 and approximately the same number of replacements built. By the evidence of the 1931 census alone it was clear that this sort of progress was not even keeping pace with the problem.

A survey of the incidence of overcrowding – defined as the use of one bedroom by children of opposite sexes above the age of ten – showed that 5·1 per cent of local-authority houses and 3·7 per cent of privately owned houses were defective in this respect. Multiple occupation was the lot of over half the citizens of London, and in Glasgow 40 per cent of the population lived more than two to a room. A further disturbing factor emerged with the discovery that modest figures of population increase since 1918 did in fact mask a considerable increase in the number of separate families. Between 1921 and 1931 this increase had statistically absorbed the entire output of new houses.[2] Moreover, the results of an analysis of income distribution indicated not only that it was unlikely that the provision of low-cost housing could ever again become profitable, but also that a significant proportion of the working population would require subsidized housing in perpetuity as their incomes could not be

(29) British housing in the 1930s. The speculatively built semi-detached villas (29) which in the form of ribbon development constituted two-thirds of the dwellings built between the wars, contrast strongly with the emerging image of a proper architecture for mass housing (*see overpage*).

expected to rise.[1] Thus local authorities had gradually assumed responsibility for a problem whose magnitude was only to become evident *after* the political commitment to its solution had been given. In the great aim of housing the poor people of Britain the traditional housing motives of profit and self-help – although still strong and with their most spectacular growth still ahead of them – had been subordinated to the idea of an open-ended government responsibility to supply housing *as a service*. Unfortunately the major evils against which this effort had been directed – overcrowding, slum dwelling and the denudation of the countryside had not only proved intractable but had been joined by new problems which were, as it then seemed, the consequence of too little development rather than too much. As in France housing estates, ranging in size between 25,000 and 100 houses, had been built on the outskirts of existing towns without urban services of any kind. Shops, adequate transport and community facilities were almost wholly absent. The image of the nineteenth-century garden city was adopted without its substance. The 4 million dwellings com-

pleted between the wars radically changed the lives of many people, but in the end inconclusively. Among planners, architects and social commentators fanatical opponents of the type of housing provided were rare; very little uncompromisingly modern housing had been constructed and the traditionally derived 'self-contained cottage' proved incapable of exciting genuine ire in progressive and conservative alike. Worthy but undistinguished housing for the 'working classes' (the term was not dropped officially until 1949) accorded with the socialist spirit of the times. As a consequence the spectacular traditional backlash of the last years of the Weimar Republic – spattered with slogans such as 'Flat Roofs, Flat Heads', illustrated by cunning photomontages of palm trees, camels and Bedouin dotted about the Weissenhof Siedlung, and justified by specious comparisons between the neglected backs of modern apartment buildings and the grand façades of the country retreats of nineteenth-century tycoons[2] – failed to find a footing in the prevailing porridge.

The few examples of modern housing that

1 G. C. M. M'Gonigle and J. Kirby. *Poverty and Public Health* Gollancz, London 1936, which indicates that some tenants on new council estates were starving themselves in order to pay the higher rents

2 Miller Lane

(30) The Guinness Trust flats, built with a nursery school on the site of a gas works in Ladbroke Grove, London.

(31) Quarry Hill flats, Leeds.

Both these developments, and some carried out in Manchester (37), lean heavily on French and German experience – particularly in the adaptation of structural systems.

were completed in the late '30s: the Guinness Trust flats at Ladbroke Grove, London; Quarry Hill at Leeds, and the quasi-modern five-storey tenements built in Birmingham and other large cities, were not associated in the mind of the British public with a new technique to solve the housing problem, but with the grudging and piecemeal release of the 'New Jerusalem' promised twenty years before. To the majority of administrators as well as potential occupants, modern design looked expensive (which it was) and seemed largely irrelevant to the central problem, at the time taken to be the dismantling of slums and provision of salubrious, low-density housing. The garden-city lobby which, apart from the large-scale suburbs of Wythenshawe, near Manchester (which interestingly enough boasted a German Beer Garden), and Becontree on the outskirts of London,[1] had been conspicuously unsuccessful in its efforts to direct the overall scale and content of municipal development, began to make itself heard again as the war clouds gathered once more.

Against all the advice of the planners,[2] the rural population was still flowing to the cities. The growth of suburbs was more than offset by a parallel increase in the number of families wanting homes, and slum clearance became a treadmill incapable of gaining ground. Perhaps the answer was a deeper and more comprehensive drive for decentralization, using government money to avoid the unbelievably slow growth of Letchworth and the financial instability of its 1919 successor Welwyn – whose constitution had collapsed in 1934 as a result of the impact of falling prices on its fixed interest security.

The problem needed to be seen clearly, so that the misconceptions and disappointments of the years since 1919 could be avoided in future. Perhaps universally low densities, a clearly two-dimensional pattern of land use, and a further proliferation of the popular 'self-contained cottage' could bring population back to the land, unravel the seething mystery of the cities and at last allow the planners to see what was really going on. A report[3] on the feasibility of such sweeping proposals was commissioned by the government in 1938, concerned for the vulnerability of urban industry and urban populations to air attack – a weakness currently being demonstrated by the Spanish Civil War. By a series of historical coincidences – not the least of which was the advent of the 'blitz' at approximately the same time as the report was published – this document became the blueprint for belated official adoption of the garden-city idea.

1 Both Wythenshaw and Becontree were designed for a population of 25,000

2 Their previously advisory status had been given the force of law by the Town and Country Planning Act of 1932.

3 *Report of the Royal Commission on the distribution of Industrial Population* (The Barlow Report) HMSO, London 1940

USA

The America to which Weimar housing experts great and small repaired from 1933 onward was itself barely emerging from a catastrophic depression uncushioned by social security legislation of the type which the Industrial Revolution had brought into existence throughout Europe. The USA with its open frontier and limitless space had absorbed the population concentrations resulting from industrialization without the widespread misery the process had brought to Europe. Small communities with little or no administrative structure had achieved high levels of productivity all over the country by means of electricity rather than steam power. The power of capital and enterprise was immense, that of state and federal administration weak; thus when the overloaded stock market crashed in the autumn of 1929, there was little to contain or mitigate the consequences. The collapse of the prosperity which had led the federal government to 'get out of housing' in 1919 brought with it direct repercussions in the form of massive mortgage foreclosures, the figures leaping from 68,000 in 1926 to 250,000 in 1932. Homelessness, poverty and public unrest reached totally unexpected heights with unemployment escalating from a conservatively estimated 6 million in January 1931[4] to a popularly quoted[5] 10 to 15 million in the following year. A hastily

4 *International Unemployment: A study of fluctuations in employment and unemployment in several countries 1910–1930* International Institute of Industrial Relations (IRI), The Hague 1932

5 *Everybody's Book of Politics* Odhams, London 1937

(32) The public sector in the United States. Lacking the right of compulsory purchase as understood in Europe, and having come into existence as a result of mortgage guarantee procedures rather than efforts to duplicate the work of the private sector, the various United States housing agencies operated on a different basis to those in Britain or Europe. These houses built in the late '30s by the Farm Security Administration illustrate both the radically different scale of the problem in the United States and the results of a native timber building tradition unhampered by traditional styling.

1 This was created by the Housing Act of 1937.

convened Presidential conference on home building and home ownership resulted in twenty-eight states enacting moratoria on mortgage foreclosures, and the establishment of a federally financed Home Owners Loan Corporation (HOLC). This latter step, although too late to save over 1·5 million mortgages, stabilized a further million by means of fifteen year loans at 5 per cent interest. Between 1937 and 1940 12 per cent of outstanding mortgages were maintained by HOLC loans. Nonetheless, during the decade 1930 to 1940, mortgage foreclosures almost kept up with the annual output of 270,000 new homes: even in 1940 foreclosures were still being carried out at a higher rate than in 1926. Conscious that some form of financial guarantee was necessary to bring investment capital into such a dubious market, the federal government created the Federal Housing Administration (FHA) in 1934. Empowered to guarantee up to 90 per cent of the cost of dwellings which could be built for $6000 or less, the FHA insured a further three-quarter of a million mortgages before the American entry into World War II. Efforts to stimulate the construction of homes to rent were less successful, with only 35,000 completions. Much admired in Europe, both pre-

and post-war, the FHA guarantee system, operating at 5 per cent interest, was one of the most successful house-financing systems introduced between the wars. Lacking both the tedious local-authority involvement of the British subsidy system, and the un-popularity of the savage *Hauszinsteuer,* it protected the free market status of American housing at a time when almost all other nations had adopted direct public-sector intervention. When the federal government did attempt such direct intervention with the ill-fated Housing Division of the Public Works Administration, which was supposed to initiate a nation-wide slum clearance pro-gramme, the courts denied the PWA rights of condemnation and compulsory purchase and a mere 22,000 dwellings were completed, most of them after the organization was taken over by the United States Housing Authority (USHA)[1]. USHA was supposed to loan money to state-established local housing authorities for the provision of low-rental housing for those who had no hope of home ownership. In 1937 only fifteen states had a legislative basis for the establishment of such authorities, while the requirement that one slum dwelling should be demolished for every USHA dwelling erected ensured that progress was slow. In the event, a proper legislative basis for US local-authority housing activities was not achieved until after 1945 – by which time changing circumstances had already led to the denunciation of publicly financed housing as 'creeping socialism'.

By 1939 between eight- and twenty-years experience of publicly financed housing in America and Europe had not brought the housing problem any nearer solution. Politicians were learning the hard way that all 'housing targets, programmes and policies are always provisional and always superseded before long'.[1] Several million dwellings had been built in Europe between 1918 and 1939 and yet new accommodation had barely kept pace with war damage, slum clearance and the increase in the number of families. Only the thought of what might have happened between 1929 and 1932 if no housing programme had been enacted served to still the tongues of western cynics and prevent them from proving, beyond a shadow of a doubt, that publicly financed housing was a waste of time.

The battle between traditional and modern design remained (outside Germany) largely a matter for the architectural propagandist, regarded as irrelevant to the serious business of housing. In a book published in 1929 on 'small modern English houses', the author, F. R. Yerbury, doubted that 'the very "advanced" type of house which is being built in some countries . . . is likely to find a place in England'.[2] Even as late as 1936, C. Leslie Wood, in a study of 'the development of the highly organized system which governs home life in the twentieth century'[3] wrote of domestic architecture, '. . . no distinctive style has evolved, unless one is to count the modernistic geometrical designs which have made their appearance here and there since the war . . . (and) . . . it hardly seems probable that these are anything more than experimental essays'.

1 D. V. Donnison *The Government of Housing* Penguin Books, London 1967

2 F. R. Yerbury *Modern English Houses* Gollancz, London 1929

3 C. Leslie Wood *As you Were* W. L. Clifford & Co., London 1936

(33, 34) Workers' houses built at Silver End, Braintree, Essex 1929 for the employees of the Crittall Manufacturing Company Ltd. Houses of this type were extremely rare in Britain at this time and the Silver End development – which still exists – represents one of the first attempts to adapt the forms of the modern movement to the purpose of low-cost housing. Architects: Sir John Burnet and Partners.

(35, 36) 'Et la guerre Aérienne?' Le Corbusier's 'Ville Radieuse' project of 1930 contained explicit reference to the dangers of aerial warfare as well as claims that most of his famous 'five points of modern architecture' were relevant to safety during modern war. According to him, large apartment blocks raised on *pilotis* would allow poison gas to flow beneath them: purified air could be sucked in from higher up. In the same way the widely dispersed *superbloques* would offer a smaller target to bombers and could in any case be armoured on top. Their concrete-frame mode of construction would also be far stronger than conventional housing. All these advantages are graphically illustrated in Le Corbusier's own sketches (35, 36). In a sense, Le Corbusier took the opposite view to most other modern architects and his enthusiastic enlistment of the dangers of Armageddon as a further piece of propaganda for modern architecture seems without parallel. Most of his contemporaries merely saw bombing as a potentially efficient means of clearing the ground.

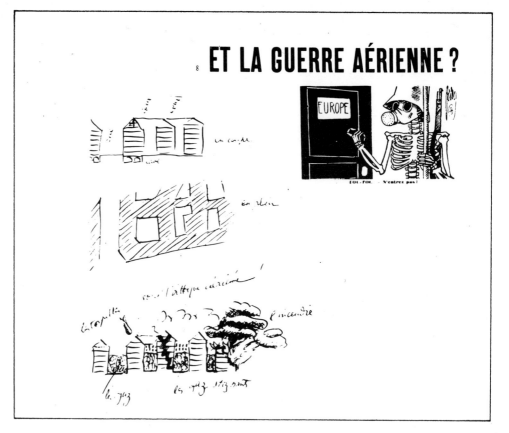

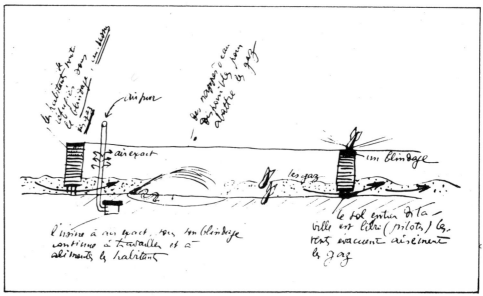

4 Bombers are a plan's best friend

'This time we know better . . . We have . . . thanks to German bombers, a much
greater opportunity for physical reconstruction.'
Lord Balfour, 1941

'One ton of bombs dropped on a built up area . . . turns 100–200 people out of
house and home.'
Lord Cherwell, 1943

'. . . the moment has come when the question of bombing of German cities . . .
should be reviewed. Otherwise we shall come into control of an utterly ruined land.
We shall not . . . be able to get housing materials out of Germany for our own needs
because some temporary provision would have to be made for the Germans themselves.'
Winston Churchill, 1945

It came as a surprise to find that the link
between planning and destruction (which can
be traced from Nero's precipitate 'slum
clearance' of AD 64 to Haussmann's 'strategic'
replanning of Paris in the 1860s), became
so very clear during the opening years of
World War II. Many architects and planners
in Britain, if not elsewhere in Europe, in-
stantly grasped the possibilities of air bombardment as a generator of opportunities
unmatched since the Great Fire of London
in 1666. Every morning during the 'blitz'
winter of 1940/41 planners scanned and
photographed the vistas opened by each

(37) Preparations for war
occupied housing authorities
all over Europe after the
Munich crisis of 1938. This
shows Manchester
Corporation flats, built
using the Mopin system
employed at Quarry Hill,
with air-raid shelters filling
the inner courts. Le
Corbusier's idea of
armouring the flat roofs
was never tried.

1 Author's italics

2 G. and E. G. McAllister *Town and Country Planning* Faber and Faber, London 1941

3 *When We Build Again* Bournville Village Trust, Allen and Unwin, London 1941

4 Maxwell Fry *Fine Building* Faber and Faber London 1944

5 J. Tetlow and A. Goss *Homes, Towns and Traffic* Faber, London 1965

6 'There is no need to consider the basis even of a most primitive existence any longer. On the contrary, it is better to destroy that, and to destroy it ourselves. The nation has proved itself weak and the future belongs solely to the stronger Eastern nation.' Adolf Hitler: March 1945. Speer, Nuremburg Trials NP. part XVII.

7 '. . . the bombs . . . have only smashed the prison walls . . . In trying to destroy Europe's future the enemy has only succeeded in smashing its past; and with that everything old and outworn has gone.' Goebbels, 'The Year 2000' *Das Reich* 23 Feb 1945

8 D. V. Donnison *The Government of Housing* Penguin Books, London 1967

successive night of bombing – before burning midnight oil at drawing boards and typewriters drafting the outlines of new cities and social orders.

In a book published in 1941 it was admiringly reported that '*while directing relief operations*[1] after the bombing of Coventry, the city architect, Mr D. E. Gibson [later Sir Donald Gibson, Director of Research and Development at the Ministry of Public Building and Works], yet found time to point out to a friend, indicating this devastated area or that, the site of a new town hall, a new school, a new shopping centre'.[2] Prefacing a book on the proposed reconstruction of Birmingham published in the same year[3] Lord Balfour expressed the same sentiments. The Minister responsible for resolving the problems of reconstruction spoke of the bombing as having 'merely given a new urgency to the problem of national planning', while one of the architects of the Modern Architecture Research Group (MARS), busy replanning London along linear principles, wrote darkly of the manner in which 'the bombs . . . knowing nothing of immutable laws except perhaps those first formulated by Newton . . . blew a whole silly theory sky high with the blast'.[4] The theory in question being presumably that of the 'natural' growth of towns as opposed to their 'planned' development. As late as 1965 planners reminisced about 'the atmosphere of enthusiasm for planning which was universal during the War, when our cities were nightly and daily being attacked by high explosive and incendiary bombs'.[5]

Hitler himself (when Germany in turn received 'opportunities for physical reconstruction' which made the bombing of London and Coventry look like the work of children), endeavoured to extend the range of destruction so as to provide more comprehensive ashes from which the Phoenix of the new Europe could arise.[6] Goebbels too saw a clear connection between the destruction of the old Germany and the inevitable failure of the war aims of the allies.[7] Today, in terms which are never wholly ironic, the economic success of Germany and Japan is attributed in part to the opportunity to 'start again' which environmental destruction afforded

them, while Professor Donnison, comparing the post-war housing performance of selected European countries,[8] refers ruefully to the benefits Germany accrued from the 'housing policies of the RAF and USAAF'.

The dramatic course of the first two years of the war, however, ensured that of all the major European contenders for housing supremacy, Britain was the only one in any position to consider planning of the kind her architects enthused over. France fell in the summer of 1940, following Poland, Denmark Belgium and Norway into German hands. In the following year, after seizing Greece from the failing hands of his incompetent Italian

(39) Terraced houses destroyed by bombing in Cambridgeshire, 1941. Throughout the war, and with increasing efficiency, bombing was used as an anti-housing weapon by both sides.

ally, Hitler invaded the USSR and within a year had penetrated deep into European Russia, obliterating all housing in occupied areas and undoing at a stroke the desperate remedial measures of the *Standargilstroi*. Britain, faced with siege from the air, remained free from invasion: the only remaining combatant democracy able to plan, design and build.

It was soon apparent that her housing losses would be severe – if only as a result of non-

(40, 41) Berlin, May, 1945, after occupation by the Russians. Over 40 per cent of the pre-war accommodation in the city was completely destroyed – another 20 per cent was temporarily or permanently uninhabitable. Nearly 2·5 million dwellings were destroyed in Germany out of a pre-war total of just under 10 million.

construction during the war years. This impending crisis was foreseen and the government made some effort to adapt the forthright methodology of the war effort to deal with it. The solution was to be on two levels: strategic dispersal of urban populations, and the accelerated construction of emergency dwellings during the immediate post-war period. This composite plan was to exert a powerful influence on British housing policy for the next quarter of a century, particularly on the strategic plane where its basic principles were set forth in the Barlow Report published in 1940. Commissioned in 1938 as an investigation into the social, economic and strategic implications of

49

1 A. and E. G. McAllister *Town and Country Planning* Faber and Faber, London 1941

(42, 43) The development of mass-production techniques for automobiles – largely pioneered by Henry Ford – had a profound effect on the course of modern architectural theory. Walter Gropius (writing in *American Architect and Architecture* February 1938) quoted figures which showed that between 1913 and 1926 the average cost of building a house in the United States had increased by 200 per cent, while the cost of cars had *fallen* by 22 per cent, and the cost of Ford cars by 50 per cent. During the same period the cost of living had risen by 178 per cent. It is thus hardly surprising that architects should endeavour to repeat this success by industrializing building. Reasons for the failure of this dream are discussed later, but the powerful imagery of the Ford production line set up for the Model A (after a six-month close down) in 1927 (42), and the thinking evident in the prototype line (43) set up fourteen years earlier, still represents an unanswered challenge to the modern architect a generation later.

industrial conurbations, the report recommended decentralization, dispersal of industry, construction of new garden cities, suburbs, satellite towns and zoned light industrial areas. The new Minister of Public Building and Works, Lord Reith, enthusiastically endorsed the report's advocacy of drastic planning controls, which, in a separate minority conclusion, amounted to support for the establishment of a Ministry of Decentralization combining the general planning powers of the Ministry of Health with unique powers over specific areas, selected for redevelopment or the building of new towns. Reith himself favoured the idea but in the event German bombing proved the most persuasive advocate of the scheme and successfully 'banished the last arguments against decentralization'.[1] Thus, although the called-for ministry was not in fact set up at that time, a combined committee of the London County Council and the six counties surrounding London was formed in 1942 and charged with the preparation of a plan for the Greater London Area under the control of Reith's nominee, Sir Patrick Abercrombie. The Greater London Plan which emerged from this study incorporated the original Barlow recommendations but went further, proposing actual sites for between seven and ten new towns intended to absorb London's 'excess' population.

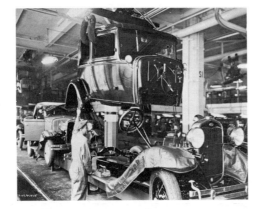

The emergency housing arm of the recovery programme developed in a more complex fashion, requiring a certain digression from the main theme of this narrative in order to describe it adequately.

Ever since 1923, when Le Corbusier first compared the Parthenon with a motor car, gloomy comparisons between the performance of the automobile industry and the building industry had been part of the stock in trade of the modern architectural theorist. Six cars could be built in 1924 for the price of one in 1904[1] while the same period had seen only a steady rise in the cost of housing. Designs for low-cost and prefabricated houses abounded in the '20s and '30s, but only in America, where before 1934 no state-subsidized housing existed, did they achieve any real success. Explanations for this European failure ranged from complaints about the deadening conservatism of those organizations capable of financing housing on a large scale, through learned dissertations on the 'biological' dissimilarity of housing and automobiles,[2] to Le Corbusier's frank statement that in the public mind the purchase of a house was equivalent to writing one's will[3] and consequently the correct state of mind for the acceptance of mass-produced housing did not yet exist.

In America experiments with prefabricated and temporary housing were carried on continuously from the mid-nineteenth century, when the Chicago-originated 'Balloon' frame technique of timber construction (using wire nails for jointing and assembly) accustomed local craftsmen to working speedily with pre-cut timber. By 1900 many systems had been developed for farm buildings and houses consisting of pre-packaged studs, girths, sheet partitions and fittings, together with simple assembly diagrams. However, very few systems achieved volume production, and none reached the figures recorded for the Weir and Dorlonco, two experimental types of house built in Britain. Nonetheless the large-scale demographic changes brought about by population migration and public works projects like the Tennessee Valley Authority (TVA) scheme maintained a consistent though small market for the type of construction useful under these conditions.

(44) Buckminster Fuller's Dymaxion house project of 1927 which employed high strength alloys, plastics and tensile structural techniques was a staggeringly advanced conception. The designer claims that volume production could have reduced the price to $3000 per unit – a figure only slightly higher than that achieved by the war-time Quonset house (51).

As motor vehicles became more widely used the size of component units was increased and at length pre-assembled wall and floor units gave way to complete or sectional houses. Buckminster Fuller for example designed a prototype mass-production, light alloy, air-freightable house in 1927, which incorporated air conditioning, plumbing, kitchen and bathroom units in a central structural mast. This project, which continues to astound successive generations of architects by virtue of its usurpation of almost all the *avant garde* thrones of the next forty years, was intended at the time to sell for $3000, provided volume production could be maintained. The following decade saw a series of prefabricated house systems being offered on the American market, backed up by numerous bathroom and kitchen units and culminating in the Hobart, Van Ness and Le Tourneau houses which were completely factory-made and delivered whole to the site. The Tennessee Valley Authority itself produced a sectional truckable house in 1939 which could be delivered economically over a radius of sixty miles. In the same year two American architects, Goldberg and Black, designed a prefabricated, mast-supported, portable ice-cream kiosk – the only true heir to Buckminster Fuller's Dymaxion I.

In Britain there were no notable efforts at

1 F. R. S. Yorke *The Modern House* Architectural Press, London 1934

2 Maxwell Fry *Fine Building* Faber and Faber London 1944

3 Le Corbusier *Towards a New Architecture* (Tr. Frederick Etchells) Architectural Press, London 1927

producing temporary housing after World War I and all prefabricated work was directed at overcoming the shortage of skilled craftsmen which dogged the country for a decade. The chief concern was with the production of permanent, low-cost, subsidized dwellings, so naturally durability and simplicity were the chief requirements. The means employed were steel and reinforced concrete, both materials whose potential as building components had scarcely begun to be developed. The Weir House, for example, over 1500 of which were completed in 1927, employed hot rolled steel sheets of a very heavy section, originally manufactured during the war for shipbuilding; while the Dorlonco House (10,200 completions), used a steel frame clad in rendered metal lathing. Of the

concrete houses the Boot Pier and Panel Continuous Cavity House (9000 completions between 1926 and 1929), featured pre-cast columns running the full height of the house at narrow centres with concrete block walls set between; while the Waller House, built of those large pre-cast wall units which the Germans termed *Massivblock*, failed to get into production at all – owing to the cost and complexity of the site organization required. All these designs without exception faithfully imitated the form of conventional semi-detached villas to an extent which gravely compromised even the economic advantages their novel means of construction were supposed to represent. Their success was also inhibited in some cases by efforts to employ cheap unskilled

labour in their erection, which led to union action.

By 1930 the economic conditions which had led to the construction of these houses no longer existed; as a result of the Depression more than sufficient labour was available for construction work and all experiment ceased. For this reason the coming of war in 1939 found Britain without the native resources to exploit the sudden arrival of a market for dwellings which could be rapidly produced without reference to the usual problems of land ownership, finance, building legislation or contractual delay. She chose to provide hostels rather than houses for the thousands of conscripts – a decision which in retrospect can be seen to have had far reaching consequences for the future of housing in Britain and Europe during the post-war period.

In Germany, where experimental work on prefabrication had been much more advanced in the '20s, a similar situation prevailed but for quite different reasons.

At Frankfurt May had designed whole suburbs to be constructed in pre-cast concrete systems of the *Massivblock* type mentioned above. Site organization was carefully arranged so that there was no repetition of the Waller House fiasco, and the planning of the

(46) The Hobart transportable house, 1938. The neo-Georgian appearance is curiously un-American in view of the steel-frame construction and the uncompromising modernism of the contemporary TVA truckable house (45).

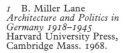

(47) The Weir house, developed by the Cardonald Housing Corporation, was basically a timber frame clad in heavy steel sheeting originally rolled for ship production during the Great War. Equipped with a felt insulating membrane and fibreboard inner skin, some 1500 were completed in Scotland during 1927. Development was in response to the serious shortage of craftsmen and raw materials felt after 1918. Note the slavish imitation of the appearance of a brick built 'self-contained cottage'. All British experiments in prefabrication laboured under this disadvantage until the 'Emergency Factory Made' programme of 1944.

1 B. Miller Lane *Architecture and Politics in Germany 1918–1945* Harvard University Press, Cambridge Mass. 1968.

2 A Bauhaus design for a corrugated copper sheet house employed the same technique. See Walter Gropius *The New Architecture and the Bauhaus* Faber and Faber, London 1935.

suburbs took account of the necessary movement of the cranes which were to locate the large elements. The use of steel in German prefabrication was greatly increased by the steel glut of 1927, when the huge *Vereinigte Stahlwerke* put a great deal of effort into marketing steel houses. Although only a small number were actually constructed many technical problems were overcome at the prototype stage. However, Hitler's accession to power in 1933 and the denunciation of the modern housing projects of the Weimar Republic as 'stationary sleeping cars . . . the work of the nomads of the metropolis who have lost entirely the concept of the homeland, and no longer have any idea of the "house as inherited, as a family estate"'[1], brought a rapid end to all

but military development of low-cost enclosure.

In Vienna a prefabricated metal house was developed by Josef Hoffmann which employed light steel sheet, corrugated for strength in the same manner as the contemporary Junkers airliners.[2] This method, like that advocated for Le Corbusier's *maisons rurales* in 1927, compared favourably with the heavy steel sheet construction employed on the Weir House in Britain, but because of inadequate market research, undercapitalization and a misunderstanding of the real strength of public resistance to *insubstantial looking* forms of housing, neither project had even the modest success of the humble British equivalent. The dream of housing

(48) Le Corbusier, project for metal *maisons rurales*, 1927. Like Buckminster Fuller, Le Corbusier strove to adapt the most advanced structures (aircraft, automobiles) to the needs of housing. In Britain and Germany the basic inspiration was different and the products notably more massive.

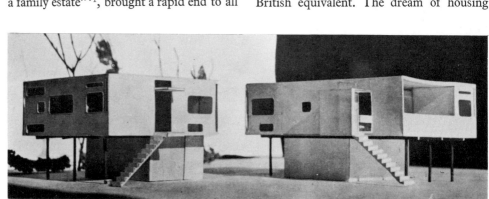

produced like automobiles was nowhere realized.

Thus, when faced by mobilization, America alone was in a position to deal with the task of finding emergency accommodation for the thousands of conscripts by means of large-scale defence housing projects. Approximately 9 million workers were rehoused in two years, the majority of them with their families – a migration considerably larger than that which took place in Britain.

Apart from her less desperate strategic position America possessed considerable natural assets to aid her in this enormous task. Raw materials of all sorts, including unlimited supplies of home grown timber, were in relatively plentiful supply, and the absence of Federal housing subsidies until the mid-1930s had encouraged the development of low cost, short life dwellings.

By 1942 when all the Federal housing agencies were consolidated into the National Housing Agency (NHA), prefabrication was able to play a large part in the wartime construction of over 850,000 dwellings. Whole townships such as the 5000 unit Willowcourt – built to serve the Willow Run aircraft plant, McLoughlin Heights, near Washington – and the 10,000 unit Portland, a township built to serve the Kaiser Shipyards in Oregon, were produced using the timber, steel and alloy techniques derived from many years of pre-war experiment. A twin-drum dwelling was devised by Buckminster Fuller from standard steel grain bins and production rose to 1000 units per day. Designed to serve as radar station, dormitory or field hospital, the unit was also used to house aircrew in transit in the Middle East.

A continual stream of information about these developments reached Britain as a consequence of Lend-Lease (the arrangement by which she received large quantities of munitions on deferred payment terms), and the arrival in England of growing numbers of American troops with their own base facilities, including prefabricated barracks, airfield construction plant and wholly new techniques of supply and servicing.

(49) 'Willowcourt', a 5000 unit Defence Housing project built to serve the Willow Run aircraft factory in 1944. The plywood houses were completely prefabricated and trucked to the site intact. American expertise in emergency housing derived from the presence since the nineteenth century of a native tradition of timber prefabrication, together with a market for short-life cheap housing, itself probably stemming from the absence of any significant publicly financed housing policy until the late '30s.

1 *Tomorrow's Houses* ed. John Madge, Pilot Press, London 1946.

Such was its effect that even in 1943, when it was variously calculated that between 4 and 5 million houses would have to be built in Britain during the first ten years of peace, the question of temporary housing was raised again. This time consideration was given to the idea, emanating from the war industries themselves, that some of the industrial capacity devoted to the construction of military vehicles and aircraft could be diverted after the war into the construction of houses, using materials and techniques not previously employed. The key aim was to diversify the raw materials of housing and at the same time bypass the seemingly inevitable dependence upon skilled building labour which had so gravely handicapped post-World War I reconstruction. Only two of the experimental houses of the '20s, the Weir Cardonald and the Telford, had been developed outside the construction industry: this time – as Lord Balfour might well have said – Britain was going to learn from her mistakes.

Special committees from the automobile and aircraft industries were rapidly convened and design work commenced, to be given added point by a new German onslaught in the summer of 1944, this time using flying bombs and, later, rockets. At once work was expanded and thrown open to public inspiration to such effect that by the end of 1945 nearly 1400 methods of construction were submitted to the Ministry of Works; of these eighty-three were deemed sufficiently interesting for prototypes to be authorized and about twenty went into production in large or small numbers.[1] The pressed steel house which resulted from the activities of the automobile-based design group was exhibited in 1944 and christened the 'Portal' after the then Minister of Works Lord Portal. It was later joined by the 'Arcon' asbestos-clad house (of which 46,000 were to be built), and finally by the aircraft industry based Airoh house, which achieved a production of 54,000 units, at one time at the rate of one every twelve minutes. Steel-frame two-storey houses developed at the same time included the British Iron and Steel Federation (BISF) house – of which 36,000 were later ordered, and the Braithwaite house: the prototype of which was destroyed by a German flying bomb late in 1944. These latter two formed

(50) An American prefabricated plywood house, the 'Pilot', exhibited in 1945 as a possible auxiliary for British housing recovery. In the event, few United States houses were imported into Britain although many were used on the Continent.

(51) The Quonset house, comprising four rooms with radiant heating, plumbing, bathroom and kitchen with gas water heating and refrigerator: all inside 500 sq. ft for a price of $2500. Manufactured by the Great Lakes Steel Corporation this converted military hut was produced in enormous numbers and shipped to all parts of the world.

(52) Arcon asbestos-clad prefabricated emergency houses in use. Well designed and equipped, these dwellings – of which 46,000 were erected – were intended to absorb surplus munitions productions capacity at the end of the war. In the event labour costs proved prohibitive and for this and other reasons the original order for a quarter of a million emergency dwellings of all types was cut back to 150,000. Production was stopped altogether in 1948.

an interesting bridge between the single-storey, American inspired emergency dwellings, and the traditionally built 'self-contained cottages' which were – as before – to form the backbone of the post-war housing effort.

If the public gloom and professional misgivings which greeted such attempts as the government made to popularize 'prefabs', seem in retrospect to smack of ingratitude, this is because the solid virtues of permanence and respectability – then as later – revealed unexpected depths. Soon living in a 'prefab' came to be regarded as only one stage better than being a 'squatter' – one of the 39,000 illegal occupants of disused army camps who forced the government to temporarily legitimize their tenure in 1946. Lack of public enthusiasm was, however, probably irrelevant to the final economic failure of the prefabricated dwellings programme.

Like Buckminster Fuller's Wichita house of 1946 – a technically more advanced and far more impressive product – all the British attempts to design a bridge between the highly stressed structure and multiplicity of subsystems characteristic of aircraft production, and the low-stressed, simply serviced enclosure required for housing, failed dismally in a spiral of rising costs, labour difficulties, expensive site work and (most of all) expiring conditions of wartime urgency.

Of the 500,000 'prefabs' proposed in 1945, barely 150,000 were completed before production was stopped in 1948. The factors which militated against success in both countries were so numerous that technical disparities became insignificant and need no longer concern us. The only long-term success of these attempts to anticipate the market possibilities of some far distant future was their strength as images. Images which, combined with the dim recognition that emergency conditions created design opportunities, were to bear fruit long after the Arcon, Airoh and Wichita houses had been forgotten.

A clear understanding of the real impact of the World War II emergency housing boom on the architects and designers of twenty

(53) An Airoh aluminium house, part of the war industries production programme relating to the aircraft industry, is erected on a bombed site in London's Oxford Street in May 1945. The most sophisticated and expensive of the 'prefabs', Airoh house production reached 54,000 before termination in 1948.

(54) The first pair of Braithwaite steel frame houses being erected at Burnt Oak before their destruction by a German flying bomb in the autumn of 1944. Enough parts were later salvaged to build a single house.

years later, can best be reached by leafing through the books and magazine articles which chronicled its achievements from 1941 to 1946. Side by side with photographs of Californian defence housing towns, drenched in sunshine and crowded with cars, are the bleak, miserable products of British inter-war experiment: the depression-ridden imagery of a creatively bankrupt public sector whose slavish imitation of the 'self-contained cottage' in materials as diverse as concrete, steel and timber spoke to the student of the mid-'60s of the death of all inspiration. For him a new meaning was to be appended to the idea of a house built like an aircraft, transported by truck and plugged in and out at will.

(55) Buckminster Fuller, Wichita house, 1946. An American equivalent to the British Airoh house, this design was to have been produced in large numbers by the Beech Aircraft Corporation at the close of World War II. Cost and labour difficulties prevented the plan from proceeding beyond the prototype although 3700 units were ordered and the proposed retail price was $6500 – well below the FHA maximum for mortgage guarantee purposes.

(56) The London area decentralization proposed in the Abercrombie Greater London Plan of 1944.

N

London County Council area	Green belt
Inner urban ring	Outer country ring
Suburban ring	Railways
	Proposed new towns

5 The end of the strategic argument

'In the event of war breaking out in any part of the world we ask you to bomb as many historic buildings as possible. Most of these buildings are at present either museums of houses of prayer and are not usually inhabited. Loss of life will be minimal and your bombs will save future generations. Do not be sentimental.'

Progressive Architecture Manifesto Oxford 1961.

'On a alors prescrit . . . depuis qu'on utilisait les avions pour bombarder, une épaisseur de trente, et même parfois dans certains pays, cinquante centimètres de béton au dessus. La multiplicité des planchers de béton a contribué a la sécurité. Alors quelques chimpanzés se sont mis à crier "c'est l'art! c'est l'art!" En réalité c'était tout simplement une mesure anti-aérienne!'

Quoted by Boudon in *Pessac de Le Corbusier* Dunod, 1969.

Great Britain

The last year of World War II saw the operational use of the ballistic missile and the atomic bomb, although such was the temporal and geographical spacing of these events that few immediately saw the dreadful possibilities inherent in a combination of the two. The destruction and loss of life wrought by high explosive and incendiary bombs was sufficient at the time to confirm the increased enthusiasm of most European governments for decentralization. In Britain the destruction or evacuation of nearly 500,000 homes, the requisitioning of a further 70,000, and rent controls which had held values down to the 1939 level throughout the war, contributed to a housing situation immeasurably worse than that faced in 1918. Only increased confidence in the industrial capabilities of the nation and the landslide victory won by the incoming socialist administration served to counterbalance the gravity of the problem. Determined to approach the crisis 'as one would tackle a military operation'[1] the new government proceeded to augment its Emergency Factory Made (EFM) programme with a series of Draconian legal measures intended to clear the way for record output in the immediate post-war years when, according to wartime forecasts, 750,000 houses would have to be provided in order to compensate for damage and industrial relocation alone. Private building was virtually forbidden and the local authorities took almost the whole weight of the programme, with the exception of the New Towns scheme which was to be directly financed by the government through the agency of Development Corporations created by the New Towns Act of 1946. This part of the programme, originally intended to take population from the major urban areas – London yielding over a million[2] – by means of new suburbs and up to twenty new towns, was universally regarded as the most

1 D. V. Donnison *The Government of Housing* Penguin Books, London 1967.

2 The highest decentralization figure ever mentioned was the 1·25 million put forward by Abercrombie in the 1944 Greater London Plan. From 1945 on the figure steadily dropped for economic and strategic reasons.

(57) One of the later designs for prefabrication was the Tarran bungalow which employed a composite steel and timber frame clad in plywood/ pre-cast concrete sandwich wall panels. The bungalow could be assembled in four hours by eight men. Here Mr George Tomlinson, Minister of Works to the post-war Labour Government, is handing over the first completed bungalow to Manchester Corporation in October 1946.

(58, 59) Two of the London overspill New Towns, Harlow (61) and Stevenage (62). The type of housing built in these entirely publicly financed communities was clearly derived from a mixture of 'self-contained cottage' and 'Weimar' patterns. The Harlow flats are accompanied by a lot of housing identical to that shown in the Stevenage photograph.

1 W. G. Fiske 'Housing Needs', Paper read to the Housing Centre Annual Conference, 1957.

2 By 1958 they had contributed less than 100,000 dwellings to a post-war total of over 2 million

revolutionary proposal of all. In addition the close of 1946 saw a target for the following year of a quarter of a million dwellings, placing Britain (as in 1919) far ahead of her European neighbours in recovery.

Unfortunately history was to repeat itself more accurately still: 1947 brought a crucial shortage of materials, a serious fuel crisis and balance of payments difficulties which were to culminate in devaluation two years later. At the same time the hasty assembly of the housing programme began to reveal itself in serious defects. Requisitioning of under-used property and the production of EFM dwellings were measures acceptable enough during war and its immediate aftermath but thereafter increasingly irksome – the EFMs in particular were proving ruinously expensive. From nearly 100,000 units in 1945-6 production was cut back to less than 50,000 in 1947, then terminated entirely in 1948 with a production of only 18,000 units. As for the New Towns, although fourteen were

commissioned between 1947 and 1950, a decade would have to pass before they made any significant difference to the housing situation. Grandiloquent plans were pruned and of the million houses scheduled to be built in the first three years, barely half had been built by 1949. The census of 1951 revealed that the number of families requiring homes was almost identical to that of 1931: fourteen years of peacetime exertion had merely succeeded in marking time. The situation, plagued by economies and delays, had scarcely improved by 1956 when a new assessment of housing needs[1] revealed a crude shortage of over half a million units, not counting 150,000 families still living in caravans or limited-life dwellings. With the private sector effectively muzzled by licensing, output under the local authorities alone had failed to reach the pre-war average.

The poor housing performance of the New Towns[2] resulted in part from under capitalization and correspondingly slow growth, as

in the pre-war Garden Cities of Letchworth and Welwyn, but also derived from the political circumstances of the birth of the New Towns idea. As we have seen this plan originated in outline with the commissioning of the Barlow report in 1938, at a time when the consequences of aerial bombardment were at least as important in the minds of advocates of decentralization as were the issues of public health and urban congestion. For the next seven years the advantage offered by decentralization as a means of mitigating the effects of bombing was demonstrated repeatedly. Although also deeply concerned with good communications between dispersed industrial units, the strategist became during that time the natural ally of the Garden City and New Town enthusiast. This alliance was not confined to Britain, nor were the New Towns its sole product. In the event Russia and America both took strategic arguments for dispersed development more seriously than did Britain or any of the smaller European countries where

the advent of atomic weapons swiftly sounded the death knell of decentralization as an effective military defence.

The destructive effect of atomic bombs alone was, as we know today, enough to wipe out the small strategic advantage gained by decentralization on the scale planned in Britain, but for some time after the operational use of these weapons over Japan opinion differed as to their real capabilities.[1] During that period when, it should be remembered, Russia was not believed to possess the secret of the bomb's construction, the New Towns programme was implemented. By 1947, when the matter was settled by tests in the Pacific, the die had been cast and official justification for the New Towns henceforth employed only the arguments of reforming planners. In a New Towns panegyric published[2] in 1963 the once dominant strategic arguments were relegated to a few lines in an introductory chapter.

1 The infamous Dresden raids of February 13/14th 1945, killed 135,000 persons. An American raid on Tokyo during the night of March 9/10th 1945 killed 84,000. By comparison the 70,000 Hiroshima death toll, and the even lower figure for Nagasaki seemed at first sight to be less remarkable than was the case.

2 F. Osborn and A. Whittick *The New Towns* Leonard Hill, London 1963.

Germany

Decentralization had begun in principle in Germany as far back as 1933 when the Nazis, eager to repudiate the idea of the metropolis (wherein, according to them, the family disintegrated after three generations), launched a programme of repatriation intended to restore to the German people their roots in the land. Apart from the construction of the *Reichsautobahnen,* fast motor roads, linking

(60) A Nazi model housing development expressing their theories about a general 'return to the soil'. The Nazis' notorious anti-urbanism produced results remarkably similar to the 'self-contained cottage' idea which dominated British public-sector housing until the mid '50s. The only differences were the German inclusion of enormous garden plots to promote self-sufficiency, and a more overt – and expensive – pursuit of a rustic image.

(61) The Nazi *Autobahn* programme. A viaduct designed by Paul Bonatz and built between 1936/37. The *Autobahnen* were aspects of strategic thinking in pre-Second World War Germany where the tradition of land warfare required good lines of communication.

major population centres, little was done to implement the programme prior to 1939. The *Autobahnen* themselves no doubt foreshadowed demographic changes – but in practice dreams of colonies to the East fast overtook the original plans. As a further earnest of intentions several isolated 'demonstration settlements' of self-contained cottages (similar to the British ideal), with huge garden plots for self-supporting cultivation, were built between 1933 and 1939, but the vast majority of Nazi housing was simply a continuation of the suburban apartment development characteristic of the Weimar era. Only the radical flat-roofed variety was suppressed.

By a curious irony of fate the arcadian paradise envisaged by the Nazis was rather similar to the Morgenthau[1] proposals for the de-industrialization of Germany which the allies

(particularly France) favoured enforcing in 1945. By then Germany was in ruins: her major cities were obliterated by bombing, public utilities non-existent, currency worthless and the country itself partitioned into occupation areas. The housing situation was appalling – far worse than that of 1919. German population, despite the loss of one-third of her territory and over 5 million dead, had actually increased between 1939 and 1946 as a result of the flood of refugees and expatriate Germans which poured into the country from Eastern Europe. Of the 10 million separate dwellings listed in 1939 nearly a quarter had been destroyed in the war. In Berlin alone 40 per cent of the pre-war housing accommodation had been bombed out of existence and of the 11 million inhabitants of the ten largest cities, 6 million had left or been killed by May 1945. A *de facto* decentralization had occurred, exemplified by the 50 per cent depopulation of

1 Henry Morgenthau was Under Secretary to the US Treasury during the latter part of Roosevelt's administration. His proposals for the pastoralization of Germany after the war were never officially endorsed, but German propaganda made much of them during the closing months of the war.

66

(62) Post-war recovery housing built in East Berlin in the (former) Stalin Allee. Large areas of tiling have fallen off, betraying haste and the difficulty with which this accommodation was erected. Of the 11 million inhabitants of the ten largest cities in pre-war Germany, barely 4 million were left in the spring of 1945.

Hanover, and the 80 per cent depopulation of Munster.

However, political events were to forstall any attempt to implement the policy of dismantling German industry. Disagreements about frontiers in Eastern Europe rapidly drove a wedge between the Anglo-American and Soviet armies of occupation and within two years the former group found itself engaged in the unexpected task of hastening the formation of a Federal German Republic. After currency reforms in 1948 which established a working economy, the Republic itself was proclaimed in May 1949: the task of reconstruction which confronted it was enormous.

Relying to a great extent on American aid, and determined to pursue a strongly anti-communist political line, the new German government resolved on an entirely new approach to the housing problem and reconstruction in general. No powers of eminent domain (compulsory purchase) were invoked and no public housing was erected by government or state administrations. Instead advantage was taken of the steeply progressive tax structure inherited from the allies to encourage house building for owner occupation by means of a unique combination of government grants and loans and extensive tax relief. Up to 1955 half the money required for rebuilding could be borrowed direct from the government at advantageous terms and even today federal grants cover one-fifth of the cost of development. The enormous capital cost of this programme was covered by American and British loans, a high level of taxation and a reimposed *Hauszinsteuer*

(63) West German post-war housing. Between the end of the war and 1950 nearly 2·5 million dwellings were built or rehabilitated – despite the fact that prior to 1948 there was no recognized German currency. The development shown here replaced gutted housing in the old part of Hanover.

levied on dwellings which had escaped the war unscathed. The absence of a defence budget during the crucial early years also aided reconstruction, which from 1948 proceeded at a phenomenal rate. By 1950 the total number of separate dwellings in the country again reached the pre-war figure of 10 million – although many were still in a bad state of repair and approximately 500,000 were emergency dwellings converted from military use. The housing target for 1951 was fixed at 250,000 units, an improvement of 25 per cent over the previous two years. These figures do not however reveal the true achievement of the immediate post-war years in Germany.[1] Between 1946 and 1950 2·5 million homes were constructed, for the most part in small contracts spread all over

the country, by small builders with small resources lacking essential materials. This performance is over twice as impressive as that of Britain – and it should be remembered that currency arrangements in Germany prior to 1948 were such that neither long-term planning nor the execution of large contracts were possible until after that date.

Viewed in purely quantitative terms it seems that the absence of major redevelopment plans and the avoidance of compulsory purchase greatly aided German reconstruction.[2] The co-operatives and limited profit development companies accomplished many adjustments of ownership without complex legal arrangements, and the result was certainly no worse than that achieved in France or Britain where compulsory purchase was widely employed. None the less, the piecemeal nature of the work, deriving from the system of financing and contracting, has given German reconstruction of the early post-war years a uniquely *ad hoc* character which belies the enormous achievement it represents. Not until the late '50s, when Berlin was practically rebuilt according to splendidly monumental (and immensely expensive) competition plans, were the famous

1 Burchard notes apologetically in *The Voice of the Phoenix: Post-War Architecture in Germany* MIT Press, Cambridge Mass. 1966, that no one has yet recounted the story of German building recovery. His own book in no way makes good this deficiency – despite its title.

(64) A further example of German post-war recovery housing at Munster am Necker.

2 The absence of grandiloquent replanning is not everywhere admired. Kidder Smith (*The New Architecture of Europe* Penguin Books, London 1961), quotes the German architect Alfons Leitl on the 'fiasco of German urban reconstruction . . . a source of grim satisfaction'.

1 There is also the
manifest unpopularity of
German success stories in
most of those countries
either occupied or
belligerent during World
War II.

architects of the world involved again in German housing. The efforts of that phase lack the integrity of the pre-war *Siedlungen* and like the Weissenhof clearly reveal the unreal politics and economy (those of the isolated West Berlin) which gave them birth. The authentic achievements of 1946 to 1950 are almost all anonymous: the cumulative triumph of myriad entrepreneurial operations carried out in obscurity. For that reason, while architects and planners pay homage to Garden Cities and Unités, whose actual contribution to the problem of homelessness has been minimal, the German post-war housing effort barely receives statistical acknowledgement. The problem of style is the underlying cause,[1] for the majority of the German housing of the period was undistinguished 'self-contained cottage' work of the kind beloved by British local authority and Nazi dreamer alike. Even the urban high-rise building of the early years lacked the clarity of vision which characterized Le Corbusier's Marseilles Unité or the London County Council's estate at Roehampton, the design of which was contemporaneous with German rebuilding.

France

Just as post-war housing history had tended to repeat itself in Britain (initial burst of idealism, followed by desperate economies), and in Germany (chaos delayed start, followed by epic performance), so in France did the political confusion of the early post-war years once again delay measures essential to the provision of adequate finance for housing. A survey in 1945 indicated that approximately 1·5 million houses had been rendered uninhabitable as a result of the war. In addition 300,000 pre-war slum dwellings remained, as well as nearly half a million grossly overcrowded homes. Thus with an urgent need for nearly 2 million new dwellings, new housing arrangements were drawn up with all building controlled by licensing and all government loan finance to be approved by a government Minister. In addition numerous large-scale plans were approved for new suburbs of apartment buildings around Paris after the model of the

(65) American expertise in prefabrication spread with the advance of the allies during the closing year of World War II. In France, as in Britain, efforts were made to launch large-scale emergency housing programmes but the cost proved too great. This photograph shows an exhibition of American prefabrication technique held in Paris in June 1946 under the auspices of the French Ministry of Reconstruction.

(66) French post-war recovery housing. Shortages of building materials were almost as severe in the formerly occupied countries as in Germany itself, and France lost over one million houses during the war. The development shown here at Sarcelles shows the remorseless pursuit of the same high-density urban image as that achieved at Drancy and La Muette before the war.

pre-war *cité jardins,* and several badly
damaged towns and cities were scheduled for
complete redevelopment according to master
plans commissioned by the government
direct. Such was the confusion which resulted from these grandiloquent measures,
and such were the economic straits in which
the country found itself, that by 1950 only
about 90,000 new housing units had been
completed, and a further 60,000 damaged
dwellings repaired. Government estimates in
that year indicated that 20,000 houses a
month would need to be built for the next
forty years in order for France to catch up

with her housing deficit and cope with for-
seeable needs.

As a result the French government diverted
additional finance to housing, offered increased tax relief to mortgage holders and
reduced minimum housing standards in
order to increase output. At the same time all
businesses employing ten or more persons
were compelled by law to set aside a portion
of their wage bills for the construction of
employees' housing.

Of the grandiloquent plans one of the few to

reach fruition was the *Unité d'habitation* of Le Corbusier built at Marseilles to rehouse families from the bombed port area. Completed in 1952 this enormous building, housing 1600 people, was intended by its designer to be a vindication of the scale of development he had proposed in his *Ville Radieuse* project before the war. Its completion was owed to the personal enthusiasm of the Minister for Reconstruction, M. Eugene Claudius-Petit.

USSR

Like Germany, Russia faced a situation in 1945 at least as grave as that of the revolutionary period. About 40 per cent of her population had lived in the area occupied by the Germans, together with 60 per cent of her heavy industry, 40 per cent of her wheatfields and 30 per cent of her livestock. A working population of 12 million had been evacuated to the new industrial regions of the interior during the German advance in 1941 and 1942, and these areas themselves had been rapidly expanded in an enormous effort to match German war production. This migration, three times larger than the labour deployment of the USA, had been carried out under indescribable conditions without specially allocated resources of any kind. Housing in the new industrial areas had barely improved since 1933 and in 1939 the average floor space per person in the whole of the USSR was still below 5 square metres: just over one quarter of the contemporary West European average. Thus the living conditions of war workers sank to a new low. Hovels built of spare wood, flattened petrol tins and railway sleepers surrounded the uncompleted elements of Ernst May's brave new world at Magnitogorsk which, already housing 140,000 people in 1939, quadrupled its population during the war years. In other cities homeless workers slept in unheated, often unglazed factories while

(68) Soviet recovery housing. The workers' estate serving the Stalin Water Board factory in Moscow. The district was completed in 1948.

(69) Soviet recovery, the second phase. These prefabricated apartment houses for industrial workers were completed in the early '60s.

shift work continued twenty-four hours a day.

As the western areas of the country were liberated in 1943 and 1944, the full extent of the damage became apparent. 32,000 factories employing 4 million workers had been destroyed together with 100,000 collective farms and nearly 5 million dwellings. 12 per cent of the 1939 population were killed or missing at the end of the war.

These appalling losses – the worst of any European combatants in World War II – are given merely as an indication of the relative scale of the housing problems faced by these nations in 1945. Britain lost 4·5 per cent of her housing, Germany 23 per cent, Russia 14 per cent. In crude terms this deficit was made good by 1948 in Britain, in Germany by 1950, and in the USSR by 1951. Additional losses resulting from non-construction add about 10 per cent to the British and German figures but rather less to those for the USSR – where housing output before the first post-war five-year plan was a comparatively low priority item. None the less the 1946 to 1951 plan, with its 42 billion rouble housing budget,[1] achieved the construction of over 4 million dwellings. This achievement is particularly remarkable in view of the fact that Russia refused in 1947 to accept aid

from the European Recovery Programme: American aid being a significant factor in housing recovery in Britain, France and Germany.

Owing to the extensive overcrowding which followed the war, the absence of consumer durables such as even then existed in the West, and the fact that inflation had made the still operative 1927 rentals absurdly low, the concept of free housing began to be discussed in 1950. This possibility, as Donnison points out, is not as fantastic as it might at first appear. Soviet standardization of dwelling types and increasing use of prefabrication of the pre-war *Massivblock* type meant that roughly the same sort of multi-storey, liftless blocks of flats were being erected all over the country. Combined with the mobility of labour, which had been a key factor in Soviet industrialization since the earliest days, this meant that standard housing could conceivably be provided as a utility service without great economic loss.

In pursuit of this idea, the most extreme to emerge from the public sector anywhere in the world, the USSR began a massive housing effort in the late 1950s which led it for a time to the position where over half the annual house construction of Europe was being carried on in Russia.

[1] This is equivalent to more than eight billion roubles per year – eight times the 1931 budget for housing.

USA

In the USA, undamaged as the country was, the sudden demobilization of 8 million men and women between September 1945 and June 1946 brought about a housing crisis similar to that created by the war itself. A Federal Housing Expediter was appointed who, with the aid of the Veterans Emergency Housing Act of 1946, reintroduced wartime housing legislation together with high housing priorities for available building materials. The re-established FHA Mortgage Guarantee system and a $10,000 cost limit on all new housing in 1946 rapidly trebled the 200,000 unit output of 1945. In addition much defence and emergency housing and some military barracks and installations were converted for civilian use so that by the end

of 1946 over a million units were either available or in the course of construction.

In 1947 a tripartite Housing and Home Financing Agency (HHFA) was formed to co-ordinate the work of the Home Loan Bank, the FHA and the Public Housing Administration (PHA). Under the HHFA annual house production rose from 850,000 units in 1947 to a record 1·4 million in 1950. The PHA programme however made very little progress, the vast majority of the 1950 output being in the form of speculative or owner-occupied housing. For this reason the Federal Housing Act of 1949 incorporated a provision for the construction of 80,000 low-rental dwellings by state public housing

(70) Post-war housing in the United States: Levittown, Pennsylvania, started in 1952, completed more than 17,000 dwellings in six years. By 1965 its population was 65,000 The entire town was built by a single developer. Public sector housing progressed more slowly.

(71) Low output of publicly owned housing has plagued the United States since the war, and what has been produced is sometimes remarkable for an incongruity and dehumanization scarcely less glaring than in Europe. This racially integrated old persons' apartment block in Indianapolis, Indiana, by architects Evans, Wollen Associates, exemplifies a marriage of the worst tendencies of both continents.

1 Michael Harrington *The Other America* Penguin Books, London 1963.

2 *Life Magazine* 16 June 1947.

3 A. B. Gallion and S. Eisner *The Urban Pattern* Van Nostrand, New York 1950 2nd ed. 1963 (author's italics).

States was to be divided into units twenty-five miles square, an industrial complex was to be located at the centre of each unit while the sides would house the working population in long strips at a linear density of 160 dwellings per mile. By this means it was hoped that the number of houses destroyed by an atomic bomb strike *anywhere* would be reduced to 500. This was felt to be a distinct improvement over the catastrophic losses inevitable under existing population concentrations: 60,000 buildings having been destroyed in Hiroshima alone.[2] Recounting this story in a book published in 1950, Gallion and Eisner still felt able to claim that it showed '*the essential qualities which render a city less vulnerable to attack from the air and long range missiles are the same qualities we desire in a decent environment in peace*'.[3] To the true devotee of the Garden City even the total destruction of the traditional matrix of civilization was not too high a price to pay for 'a decent environment'.

In Russia proposals scarcely less fanciful became for a time the basis of national planning. Aided by the compulsory industrial dispersal of the World War II, Stalin revived a 1929 dream for the assimilation of rural and urban labour conditions by means of the *Agrorody* or 'agrotowns', which were to employ large numbers of workers in huge grain factories operating along the lines of urban industry. The seamless web of agricultural and industrial towns thus produced, called 'microdistricts' and numbering approximately 30,000 people each, were to feature communal catering, cultural and educational facilities. Living accommodation was to be unusually small because after the age of seven all children were to be dispatched to special regional boarding schools. Immured in these remote settlements, lacking even automobiles for escape, Soviet workers and technicians would realize the fantasies of Stalin and Ebenezer Howard alike in a truly decentralized existence.

Neither of these plans was at all practical in the social conditions which post-war recovery brought to both nations and thus the brief liaison of strategist and planner came to an end. By the mid-1950s the development of

authorities with the aid of a fixed federal subsidy. Unfortunately the outbreak of the Korean war, with its reimposition of controls on building materials and hardening political attitude against any measure which smacked of 'socialism' caused the programme to be cut back. In the same year 33 per cent of American families were judged to be inadequately housed – in real terms between 40 and 50 million human beings.[1] By 1964 only 550,000 municipally owned low-rental dwellings had been completed.

Largely as a result of their enormous untouched reserves of land both the USA and the USSR went through a brief post-atomic phase of defensive planning before the development of today's superweapons. In America the 1947 President's Advisory Commission on Universal Military Training yielded remarkable proposals: the whole of the United

more and more sophisticated delivery systems for nuclear weapons had bypassed traditional strategic thinking altogether and given rise to a new concept of warfare in which casualties of the order registered at Hamburg, Dresden, Tokyo and Hiroshima were reduced to sub-multiples of the basic unit – one million deaths. At the same time urban planners began to fall more and more into the throes of a death struggle with the automobile.

Under these conditions even the advocates of twenty-five mile squares and *Agrorody* gave up. War games escalated into the unthinkable and in Europe plans for defence against air attack ceased to be taken seriously, except when they most obviously displayed political self-serving.[1] In America considerable fallout shelter building occurred during the late '50s and early '60s, but in general the truth slowly dawned that in future the planning of human settlement could proceed without reference to the prospect of aerial assault.

As previous chapters have shown, the impetus for mass housing was derived from the large scale demographic changes which coincided with the Industrial Revolution. Public-sector housing on the other hand was the child of two world wars. In Europe the link between the two major wars of this century and the problem of housing as now conceived is indisputable: quite apart from the obvious connection between the destruction of dwellings and their reconstruction, there was the political significance of the housing programme as a key aspect of social security,

an unfailing vote-catcher and a clear index of governmental good will. The language in which housing problems came to be discussed left little doubt as to the origin of the administrative and technical models transplanted into the older regional government structure. Quasi-military terms such as 'housing front', 'housing target', 'emergency house mark IV, V and VI', 'housing units', 'high priorities', 'output', and 'strength' testify to the origin of the great post-war housing programmes in logistics and the staff and line management structure of military life.

The gradual acceptance of the idea that for most thinkable purposes land wars of conquest in Europe could now be discounted, together with recognition of the futility of civilian air raid precautions, coincided with the dawn of a new age of affluence for the West. Recovery from World War II, facilitated by American aid and an unexampled pooling of military resources, proceeded apace in the late '50s culminating in Britain and Germany in a massive property boom. Despite its almost universal use as an economic regulator both private and public housing increased output into the '60s, and the private sector in particular – chiefly through a spectacular growth in financing facilities – consistently out-produced the public sector in Britain between 1958 and 1966. The period of 'housing affluence' thus contained saw the emergence of significant changes in financing, planning, design and density: and more fundamentally a considerable change in housing attitudes.

1 Renegade nuclear disarmers created a minor scandal in 1963 by revealing government plans for the maintenance of law and order after the feared atomic holocaust. All the occupants of RSGs (Regional Seats of Government), were to have been members of the armed forces, the police, civil servants and selected intellectuals and scientists. No elected representatives of the people were included.

(72, 73) *Superbloque* working-class tenements on the outskirts of Caracas, Venezuela, together with the shanties they were designed to replace.

6 Breakdown of a theory

'The best method in behavioural science is to recognize that no single method will do; common observation should be pitted against statistics and the results of one qualitative study pitted against another. It is better to make good sense than bad science.'

Conrad Jameson 1964.

Between 1954 and 1958, during the Pérez Jiménez dictatorship, the Venezuelan government carried out a public housing programme unparalleled in Latin American history. At a cost of $200 million, ninety-seven fifteen-storey high-rise *superbloques* were built in Caracas and the neighbouring port city of La Guaria. 180,000 slum dwellers were rehoused in these buildings whose emphasis on hygiene and public health echoed that of the Victorians in England, but whose form and architectural ethos derived from Le Corbusier and the prophets of the modern movement. This unique combination was not successful: in fact the United Nations Evaluation Report[1] on the whole enterprise claimed that 'the accompanying social, economic and administrative difficulties proved to be so serious that in effect a civil anarchy prevailed'.

That these words were not used lightly is made plain by the section of the report subtitled 'social disorganization', part of which reads:

'. . . the individual families . . . were unable or unwilling to cope with new situations and to assume new responsibilities such as having to pay rent. When social disorganization set in, individuals were driven to seek solutions of their own, which consisted in many cases of returning to the slums, and in others of behaving in the new structures in the same way as they had done in their old precarious dwellings. This was reflected in improper use of services and in the gradual deterioration of the buildings. The lack of social integration caused such serious problems of relations between neighbours that the development achieved one of the highest crime rates in the metropolitan area. The gradual, and at times violent, destruction of public and community services, such as schools, parks and green areas, shops and public offices, aroused in the service personnel a feeling of insecurity that led to the temporary suspension of some services and programmes. A large increase in the number of illegal occupancies and the number of cases of arrears in the payment of rent resulted in a situation where the investment could not be recovered, and there was a loss of control over the administrative procedures for formalizing negotiations and payments.'

Elsewhere in the report the figures for rent arrears in 1959 is given as $5 million, the number of squatting families as 4000, and the monthly maintenance and security costs as $500,000. The explosive urban situation thus created contributed to the overthrow of the Jiménez government. In the largest estate, called '23rd January', thirteen police officers were killed between 1960 and 1965.

1 'Evaluation Project of the Superblocks of the Banco Obrero in Venezuela' United Nations 1959

1 Charles Abrams
Housing in the Modern World Faber and Faber, London 1966, Chap. IX

2 Alan Lipman 'The Architectural Belief System and Social Behaviour' *British Journal of Sociology* London 1968

3 This statement was in fact first made by Herbert Greenough, an American artist and sculptor, but was employed as a slogan by Sullivan

At about the same time as President Jiménez began his ill-fated housing odyssey, the government of Nigeria launched a similarly magnificent slum clearance plan for Lagos by authorizing the clearance of seventy acres in the centre of the city. Planning to avert civil dissatisfaction by selling the cleared land (after new street layouts and services had been installed) back to the original owners at 120 per cent of the compulsory purchase price, the Lagos Executive Development Board (LEDB) took out a further social insurance policy in the form of a special housing development at Suru-Lere on the outskirts of Lagos to house the displaced inhabitants while clearance was going on. Unfortunately, by 1962 only twenty-five acres had been cleared and the cost of maintaining the displaced 11,000 occupants at subsidized rents in Suru-Lere was rising alarmingly. Worse still the original owners were failing to repurchase the cleared areas for a number of unforseen reasons: firstly because replanning had reduced the available area by one third, secondly because zoning had restricted the possible uses of the remainder, and thirdly because many of the former owners had sold their right of repurchase to outside entrepreneurs. Of the few who did repurchase most failed to rise to the occasion by building splendid new quarters: instead they constructed makeshift stalls and shops similar to those originally demolished. As a result of the failure of the repurchasing scheme to operate effectively, government grants were stopped and clearance ceased. The presence of unused land and the complaints of dispossessed owners finally forced the LEDB to permit temporary reoccupation: by the end of 1963 nearly 500 original stalls had been put back and the population of the area was crawling back to the 30,000 of 1955. During the seven years operation of the scheme £3 million had been spent (exclusive of the cost of the 'temporary' accommodation of Suru-Lere) and only £700,000 received back in repurchase. The displaced occupants themselves had merely exchanged

'a shoddy home in a convenient neighbourhood for a convenient home with a tiresome journey to work. The combination of isolation, higher expenses, and lower incomes . . . (had) forced them into a self-sufficiency alien to their traditions, and harassed by demands on their overstretched resources, once unified households had been shattered.'[1]

These two spectacular failures in housing policy are also nails in the coffin of what Alan Lipman has called 'the architectural belief system'[2]: the idea that a manipulable relationship exists between spaces, volumes, textures, micro-environment and layout – and social behaviour. This is not to say that the architects of the Venezuelan *superbloques* were solely to blame for the mayhem which succeeded their completion; nor that British trained planners were responsible for the dismal failure of the Lagos slum clearance programme to the exclusion of everyone else involved. Nonetheless, there can be little doubt that the presence of architectural drawings and models played an important part in launching both these grandiloquent projects, and that an image of the social behaviour of the occupants existed in the minds of those who authorized the schemes.

How architects achieved a reputation with official clients for being able to deal with such matters is a development which only a brief study of the evolution of the ideology with which they greeted the technological changes of the twentieth century can enable us to understand.

The cornerstone of this ideology was the theory of functionalism: the idea that the purpose of a building could, if properly understood, define its form. This theory of fitness for purpose drew its most famous slogan from the American architect Louis Sullivan,[3] who died in 1924 but left on record the famous stricture that 'form follows function' – the formalized equivalent of Taylorism in the industrial production of the early twentieth century.

Widespread adoption of this approach to design allied itself to the puritanical spirit of pioneers such as Adolf Loos ('ornament is crime') to produce the characteristic bald formalism of much *première moderne*. Opposition to this cleansing and simplifying fire proved surprisingly weak, largely because the historic basis of architectural practice on patronage did not encourage the development of large social ideas about a mass clientele but rather emphasized the *minutiae* of design for a known individual. The kind of alienation to which a truly generalized approach could lead is well exemplified by the writings of some of the fathers of the modern movement – particularly on housing. Walter Gropius for example wrote in 1924: 'The majority of citizens of a specific country have similar dwelling and living requirements; it is therefore hard to understand why the dwellings we build should not show a similar unification as, say, our clothes, shoes or automobiles'.[1] Gropius went further in 1931, dismissing the 'tendency to house the majority of the population in detached dwellings' as utopian and claiming that economic considerations alone would ensure that 'the one-family house will remain reserved for a higher stratum of the population' because the 'rented dwelling in an apartment house is better adapted to the needs of the more mobile working class', who, in any case, 'lack the time required to care for a house and garden if they are not to deteriorate'.[2]

Another facet of this dispassionate interest (to put it mildly) in the fate of the mass client was revealed by Anthony Bertram in 1938 when he 'established' in a commonsense fashion the standards of 'structural honesty' to be observed in housing:

'Different methods of construction – different techniques that is – produce different kinds of houses, different in plan and appearance, unless there is a deliberate distortion of the forms that come naturally to them. A timber-frame house is and looks different from a brick house. When builders apply stained deal laths to a brick house they are trying to suggest that it was built in a way in which it was not built. That is obvious dishonesty. But supposing, as in the more expensive bogus Tudor, the house really is a timber-frame construction, is that also dishonest? I think so: because it is not planned as a Tudor house, nor is it occupied by Tudor people.'[3]

Characterizing all opposition to this bracing view as 'an unhealthy craving for the past', Bertram went on to bewail the ignorance of the masses who 'shut their eyes to plans . . . and consider the house as a façade and a few fittings'.

This exasperated outburst probably represents the apogee of the naïve phase of modern architectural determinism: the 'mechanical fallacy' of which Geoffrey Scott wrote

1 Bauhausbucher, Vol 3, *Ein Versuchshaus des Bauhauses*, Albert Langen Verlag, Munich 1924. Reprinted in translation: Walter Gropius *The Scope of Total Architecture* George Allen and Unwin, London 1956

2 '*Das Wohnhochhaus*' by Walter Gropius in *Das Neue Frankfurt,* February 1931, Internationale Monatsschrift, Frankfurt/M. Reprinted in translation in *The Scope of Total Architecture op. cit.*

3 Anthony Bertram *Design* Penguin Books, London 1938

(74) Part of the process whereby the substance of the 'self-contained cottage' changed while its image remained constant can be seen in this illustration of a conversion carried out on pre-war local-authority houses at Southampton in 1947. The house on the extreme left is in its original condition with slate roof, small paned windows and corniced brick chimney. The conversion (centre) has post-war windows with larger glass areas, copper sheet roofing and simplified chimneys. The right hand house shows the more usual concrete tiled roof allied to post-war windows and external plumbing.

(75, 76) Post-war house construction in Britain. Interior walls are constructed in concrete blocks; the roof timbers are thinner than pre-war and joined with connectors instead of complex timber joints. Windows are timber with standardized sections, fewer glazing bars and larger areas of glass. The ground floor is concrete set directly on the ground. The roof tiles are concrete also. The contrast with pre-war practice is considerable but not obvious, as comparison with these semi-detached houses in Sheldon, Birmingham (77) built in 1939 shows.

prophetically in 1914. Ushered in by Sullivan's 'form follows function', helped along by Lethaby's interesting 'houses should be as efficient as bicycles' (1912), and finally canonized by Le Corbusier's 'a house is a machine for living in' (1923), this period in architectural theory was marked by a general lack of interest in mass housing unless it was the 'standard machine product . . . (with) balanced harmony, clean planes, exciting curves, and powerful shapes'.[1] These conditions were of course only met during the brief Weimar modern phase, and consequently the vast majority of the public-sector housing completed up to 1940 passed beneath the attention of the famous pioneers.

The simplicity of these early theories succumbed in general to the technological tidal wave of World War II, and in particular to the emergency housing programmes which followed it, with their omnivorous use of *ersatz* materials of all kinds. Writing in *angst* and with rare insight, Maxwell Fry noted in 1944:

'If the structural developments which have led to our present technical skill were to continue at the same pace into this century, at a pace that is, exceeding our capacity as artists to assimilate them, then our hopes of establishing a workable architecture would be slight.'[2]

The flourishing of 'dishonest' structural methods during the post-war period must have confirmed his worst fears. Passable imitations of 'self-contained cottages' were constructed in a variety of new materials leading within a decade to a subtle but fundamental change in the composition of the traditional public-sector house, as well as its speculatively built private-sector counterpart. Ingeniously retaining its traditional image the dwelling underwent an almost complete reconstruction. Concrete floors, block linings to cavity walls, metal windows, concrete roof tiles, light timber trusses (joined by connectors instead of craftsmanship), plasterboard, chipboard, concrete lintels, flush doors, patent partitioning systems, rationalized plumbing units, asbestos and later plastic rainwater goods, central heating, reinforced brickwork, plastic flooring, strawboard insulation, mastic sealants, polythene

damp-proof membranes, plastic emulsion paint, cheap carpeting and widespread component prefabrication, all combined to rationalize traditional construction and maintain the pace of structural evolution.

From the mid-'50s onward the issue was complicated by the arrival both of high-rise building and industrialized construction techniques. The construction of blocks of flats had always been a Trojan horse for modernism in the '20s and '30s when enthusiasts had used the difficulties of the conventional housing programme as a justification for the continued building of tenements in the cities.

In Britain a quarter of a century later even more specious arguments, based on the wastage of agricultural land resulting from decentralization and the need to maintain urban densities in the face of slum clearance programmes, which were failing to rehouse all those evicted (let alone cope with the growing numbers of families wanting homes of their own), increased the weight of opinion in favour of high-rise building. The burst of skyscraper activity which ensued enjoyed only a brief period of popularity, but it was, nonetheless, the image of sophisticated urban development most often exported to the developing nations. There, excised from the complex service industries of its countries of origin, high-rise building revealed appalling shortcomings, as we have seen.

In Britain reaction against high-rise, although it culminated in public outrage at the progressive collapse at Ronan Point in 1968,[3] came about for more complex reasons than concern for the welfare of small children playing in lift lobbies 100 ft in the air. Revelations of the real cost of building high (the British government combined housing subsidy topped £140 million in 1964), and the exposure of the scandalous disparity in construction time between public and private contracts for identical buildings, led to an official *volte face*. The public sector was switched to high density, low rise development of the kind pioneered in Switzerland and France and canonized in the form of Moshe Safdie's *Habitat*, which was a great success at the Montreal Expo of 1967.

1 F. R. S. Yorke *The Modern House* Architectural Press, London 1934

2 E. Maxwell Fry *Fine Building* Faber, London 1944

3 Ronan Point block, in South London, partially collapsed as a result of a gas explosion on the twenty-second floor in the early morning of 16 May 1968. The enquiry held to determine the cause of the accident threw doubt on the safety of the structural system (using heavy concrete floor and wall units) which had been employed. Press reaction to the disaster was exceedingly emotional and led to several attacks on high-rise development in general

(77) The development of industrialized building techniques proceeded more erratically in Britain than in other European countries such as France, Denmark and Russia, and it was not until the early '60s that the larger local authorities began to award contracts of sufficient size and continuity to justify the use of complete systems – particularly for high-rise work. The photograph shows the construction of a multi-storey block of flats in Redhill, Surrey, using a heavy pre-cast concrete panel system similar to that which partially collapsed at Ronan Point in May 1968. Before this disaster the use of system building in the public sector had been increasing (in terms of the percentage of all dwellings completed), at the rate of about 6 per cent per year.

1 K. Buytendijk *An Approach to Animal Physiology* UAP New York 1948

This *volte face* coincided with the development of a more sophisticated set of architectural theories to replace the rather discredited and simplistic slogans of the '20s and '30s. Retreating from the uncompromising moral pronouncements of their peers, a later group of theorists seized upon the demonstrable truth that a relationship exists between context and behaviour and developed a kind of super functionalism based on scientific evidence. In animal physiology, it was noted, behaviour was interpreted as action informed with meaning by the sphere of values in which it took place. In these psycho-dynamic terms actions thus became binary, being expressed in the form animal-plus-context. It did not seem more than a logical progression to say that context gave meaning to action, in fact determined it. Buytendijk wrote: 'Behaviour means replying, and we understand this reply when we observe the animal from the situation which thrusts its question upon him'.[1] Following the *Gestalt* psychologists who

the architectural belief system proceeded apace.

The problem, however, was again one of naïvety. This theoretical view of the relationship between environment and behaviour requires the broadest possible interpretation of the meaning of both terms: it becomes absurd if the term 'environment' is understood merely to mean physical surroundings, and the term 'behaviour' to mean merely physical actions. Unfortunately just such a simplistic interpretation is widespread amongst architects and lies at the heart of the 'architectural belief system'. Hole[2] explains this as follows:

'Since the architect plays a part in creating or changing the built environment, he is inevitably concerned with the relationship of human behaviour to this environment; indeed he is prone to argue in terms of simple environmental determinism: change the environment and you inevitably change people's behaviour. Architecture is then seen as a social prophylactic . . .'

That this is precisely how the majority of architects do see architecture has been clearly demonstrated by Alan Lipman in 'The Architectural Belief System and Social Behaviour', in which he quotes a housing research architect as follows:

'As architects we shape people's future behaviour by the environment we create. At all stages of the design we make assumptions about human behaviour and the success or failure of our work may depend on our ability to predict human behaviour.'[3]

Even when a more comprehensive view of environment is taken, this is no guarantee that the architect has relinquished all hope of cramming its very essence into the forms he has conceived: a housing thesis submitted to the London Architectural Association School in 1969 contained this passage:

'Abrams comments, "environment is more than physical environment, it is a combination of physical, social and

1 Roger Barker and Herbert Wright 'Psychological Ecology and the Problem of Psychosocial Development' *Child Development* Vol 20, No 3. September 1949

2 W. V. Hole 'User Needs and the Design of Houses – The Current and Potential Contribution of Sociological Studies' CIB Commission W 45, Symposium. Oct 1967. National Swedish Institute for Building Research, Stockholm 1967

3 John Noble 'The How and Why of Behaviour: Social Psychology for the Architect' *Architects' Journal* 1963, *137*, pp. 531–546

shared some of this ground, two behaviourist psychologists, Barker and Wright,[1] extended this idea into the human context by portraying human behaviour as dependent upon a 'situation' or 'setting', its own 'homeland' without which it cannot be described. The architectural relevance of this assumption is immediately obvious as it implies that the built environment must influence or even control the actions which take place within it. Barker and Wright's theory dates from 1949 and from then on the development of

(78) Two sketches showing the designed positions of furniture in a local-authority house and the positions chosen by the occupants as recorded by an observer some months after completion. The author of the report describing this disparity notes that none of the occupants of dwellings on the estate in question had placed their furniture in the designed positions so that 'we could conclude the room was too cramped for a particular furniture arrangement which never occurred' (*Architects' Journal*, 24 August 1966). That the inhabitants of the houses might have deliberately chosen *their own* furniture layout for other than utilitarian reasons does not seem to have occurred to him.

  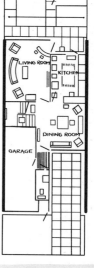 

personal factors". To these factors should be added political, psychological and economic considerations, the processes and methods of attainment as well as the goals. Housing as environment, influenced by all these forces, would be a reflection of civilization and culture, and the strategy for housing policy could not be governed by any one of these forces, such as the pure statistics of the situation, but must value all factors, *with the physical manifestation becoming part of the vocabulary through which the other considerations may be reflected.*' [author's italics]

The idea that 'physical, social, personal, political, psychological, economic, civilizational and cultural factors' can all be expressed through 'the physical manifestation' is rather like expecting Beethoven's ninth symphony to be adequately recorded on a dictaphone. The channel capacity is insufficient – the bare outline of the public-sector home is too weak a thing.

Even if it were not, there are even more comprehensive definitions of situational complexity. Anthony Ward in 'Right and Wrong' lists some difficulties involved in receiving an account of a situation:

'Meaning can only be sketchily derived

from the situation by encouraging the person to describe his feelings explicitly. Yet even when this is done, we cannot trace the meaning of his communication without including ourselves in the experiment too. We need to know not only what he feels about the situation but also what we feel about it, what we think he feels about it, what we think he thinks we feel about it; what he feels about it, what he thinks we feel about it, what he feels about it, what he thinks we feel about it, what he thinks we think he feels about it . . . The observer's experiences of the observation situation

(79) 'Personalization' – the
alteration or improvement
of his dwelling by the
occupant – is nothing new.
As a comparison between
these photographs
illustrates, the houses built
by Le Corbusier at Lège
and Pessac over forty years
ago have practically all
been modified into hybrid
structures, with pitched
roofs and narrowed
windows. Philippe Boudon,
in *Pessac de Le Corbusier*,
discusses this process at
some length and with
greater understanding than
has been applied by recent
exponents of territoriality.

Pessac, 1926

(80) Pessac, 1967

cannot be separated from the total
situation . . .'[1]

It is in this hall of distorting mirrors that the
'behaviourist' architect loses himself once he
begins to come to terms with the multi-
faceted nature of 'environment'. Small
wonder that he finds it (apparently) simpler
to use the word as a synonym for 'physical
surroundings'.

The complexities of 'environment' are
matched by similar difficulties on the other
side of the equation. Behaviour is far more
complex than it might at first appear, and
once again it is only by grossly oversimplify-
ing its meaning that the forthright tone of
'functionalist' propaganda is maintained.

The Parker Morris Report of 1961, for
example, contains the passage: '. . . the right
approach to the design of a room is, first to
define what activities are likely to take place
in it, then to assess the furniture and equipment necessary for these activities, and then
to design around these needs . . .'[2] As a consequence of this widely accepted approach
efforts to find out what people want are
always carried out via the search medium of
functional analysis, with results which can

1 Anthony Ward
'Right and Wrong'
Architectural Design, July
1969

2 'Homes for Today and
Tomorrow' report of a
subcommittee of the
Central Housing Advisory
Committee. HMSO,
London 1961

(81a) Lège, 1926

(82a) Lège, 1926

(82b) Lège, 1967

1 John Noble 'Appraisal of User Requirements in Mass Housing' *Architects' Journal*, 1966. August 24. 479–486

2 Philippe Boudon *Pessac de Le Corbusier* Editions Dunod, 1969

only define the environmental needs of the building user in the narrowest possible sense. Ostensible activity (which is often all that can be uncovered by the genial architectural inquisitor), is not the same as *behaviour*; by pretending that it is the investigator merely robs his subjects of their *experience* of environment with results which can range from the dehumanized to the bizarre. Noble[1] records a study in which the design of dwell-

ings for public-sector tenancy was finalized right down to the location of windows on the assumption that dining tables and chairs would be put in certain positions. To the surprise of the designers a visit to the house some months after occupancy revealed considerable, even perverse, furniture changes which made nonsense of the 'tight fit' of the original concept. In another, and even more spectacular, case Boudon[2] found that the

inhabitants of some of Le Corbusier's famous houses at Pessac, near Bordeaux, had bricked up the room-width windows bequeathed by the master and replaced them with bay windows. The reason given was that the original windows were 'old fashioned' and 'nowadays people prefer bay windows and leaded lights'.

Outside the domestic field further examples of the deeply limiting design solutions derived from the 'architectural belief system' command attention. Describing the planning of an electrical engineering faculty Anthony Ward points out that although 'choice, movement, structural and services criteria were optimized by computer into the most efficient possible free form which was then translated into a "building" form, in which capital and

1 Anthony Ward
'Right and Wrong'
Architectural Design, July
1969

2 Norman Mailer
Moonshot Weidenfeld and
Nicolson, London 1970

3 Probably the best and
clearest attack on the
experiments of the
'behaviourist' school was
delivered by Janet Daley in
an article entitled 'The
Myth of Quantifiability',
published in the
Architects' Journal 21
August 1968

4 Norris Kelly Smith
*Frank Lloyd Wright: a
study in architectural
content* Prentice-Hall, New
York 1966

5 Bruce Goff
Architectural Design May
1957

running costs for all criteria were at a minimum, the final product . . . was seriously limiting in terms of user choice. The user was allocated his efficient space in an efficient total structure, where *movement and choice were minimized.*'[1]

The building had become, in Norman Mailer's unforgettable phrase, 'the architectural skull for a new kind of brain'.[2]

The consequences of this lobotomized perception are limited only by the inadequacy of the original view of 'behaviour' upon which they were based. In the consideration of housing as a largely socio-political phenomenon (which has been the standpoint of preceding chapters) it has been shown that questions of design were of small significance in the general development of mass housing: economic and social factors were of greater importance. In the field of planning the design of individual units was a matter of even less concern, provided the essential decisions about density and form of development were taken. It was only with the coming of affluence and the recasting of housing in the role of principal consumer durable, that the question of design and the problem of public preference loomed large.

Just as the congestion in a manufacturing town of the Industrial Revolution revealed the inadequacies of 'natural' drainage and local water supply, so the proliferation of choices in housing and domestic equipment has revealed the blindness and deafness of the 'architectural belief system' in relation to the mass client. Proceeding from its dubious principles the 'behaviourist' architect is able to see the world in a different way to that in which he feels it. He can design a maximum security prison with as little concern as a *kindergarten* because any empathetic feeling he may have possessed is lost outside the scope of the tunnel vision forced upon him by his methodology.[3]

It would be innaccurate to suggest that this alienation is solely the result of a too literal interpretation of certain concepts in physiology and psychology. Subjective experience of the failure of the imagery of the modern

movement to compensate for unintelligible social roles and incompetent environmental administration would certainly have applied a corrective by now, if such experience had been part of the life of the average housing architect. Unfortunately it is not: from the turn of the century until the present day the role of the architect has been subtly changing, and with it his relationship to his client – and the building user.

The manner in which this change came about requires elucidation since it is not only involved with the whole development of mass housing, but also stems from the social changes which coincided with the Industrial Revolution. The role of the architect before World War I was primarily that of an artist; an interpreter of human needs on the basis of creative insight and a vocabulary of formal styles which (to the initiated) conveyed *agreed meanings.* The architect of this period required patronage in order to achieve advancement; he was in general known to his client, of a similar educational background, and party to the same social, religious and political beliefs. The extent to which this identity of interests could be *led* by the creative inspiration of the architect was often surprising. In his penetrating study of Frank Lloyd Wright, Norris Kelly Smith argues that Wright, far from being an utopian modernist, was in fact a markedly conservative and respected figure of middle-class Chicago society – his flamboyant clothes and oracular speech were accepted artistic foibles. 'From first to last Wright was concerned with . . . a social ideal of harmonious consistency. He knew perfectly well for whom he was working. He found his clientele among a class of sober and responsible businessmen, for whose taste and judgement he had considerable respect.'[4] That this tradition of moral conservatism and formal radicalism is not entirely dead is evidenced by the career of Bruce Goff, whose practice enjoys the same domestic emphasis as Wright's and is founded on a similarly solid and respectable clientele.[5] Nonetheless, outside the American Middle West the predominantly artistic, domestic and conservative bias of the practice of architecture suffered a considerable change in the early years of this century – particularly in Europe.

The abandonment of the artist's right to an unchallengeable creative impulse, which was a part of the price of this change, involved the architect bending his creation to conform to objective criteria. In doing so he relinquished an opportunity to lead the twentieth century in the sense that McLuhan has described.[1] In aping science he became vulnerable to scientific dismissal, and that is what has occurred. His functional idea, buttressed by scientistic formulae has been found an *inadequate generalization* for the complex phenomena it is supposed to contain.

Inevitable though this *dénouement* might appear in retrospect, there is little doubt that the architectural profession came to terms with the increasing power of the public sector and the increasing anonymity of the building user by degrees. Public-sector housing was always an emergency business, economies were always at a premium, red tape was always present in large quantities. In conforming to the demands which this work-environment made on them, architects slowly but surely adopted a positivist, behaviourist, objective outlook *as a means of survival*.

In Britain today over a third of registered architects are in the salaried employment of local or central government, of the remaining two-thirds the majority derive up to 30 per cent of their commissions from official sources. The official, bureaucratic ethos thus infiltrates a sizable minority of the profession, and through the agency of building regulations, public utilities and planning restrictions effectively circumscribes the activities of all practitioners. This state of affairs is alone sufficient to explain much of the current emphasis on structural and economic performance at the expense of artistic creation. Taken in conjunction with the abandonment of pupillage, the growth of government-financed architectural schools and the decline in the percentage of architects from the highest (financially independent) social strata, this drift away from creativity towards management is symbiotic with the development of public-housing agencies and the dominance of the mass (or anonymous) client in place of the patron.

Given this change from artist to environmental engineer, and from protégé to civil servant it is hardly surprising that the addition of a scientific basis to the functionalist theories of the early moderns should have proved an *administratively* successful posture. The surprising thing is that the resulting jumble of technical expertise and theoretical bankruptcy should have been so long maintained in the face of clear evidence as to its unpopularity.

Once again the answer is to be found in the history of the emergencies of the last hundred years: cholera, population explosion, World War I, the Depression, World War II, reconstruction, all are writ large in the story of Mass housing. Not until the '60s did affluence, the abandonment of conscription, patriotism and effective defence, and the birth of a kind of officially endorsed hedonism bring about a change in circumstance – and with it a new and hostile appraisal.

Architectural Review for November 1967 was devoted to a survey of British housing. Concerned chiefly with the usual architectural red herring of 'creating a total environment', a seamless web of old and new urban development, the issue nevertheless found space to express concern, obviously unfeigned, over the type of high rise, *béton brut* public-sector housing which was then in the course of construction all over the country. Heavily illustrated with photographs which looked so obviously tendentious that an editorial disclaimer ('the photographers . . . were asked to record simply what they saw in the areas they visited – neither to exaggerate the sordid . . . nor to fawn on the architectonic,') was deemed necessary, the issue afforded several opportunities to glimpse the curious amalgam of 'modern' thought and scientific mumbo jumbo underlying many massive housing developments. At Sheffield for example two large public-sector developments, 'Park Hill' and 'Hyde Park', housing between them over 2000 families on fifty acres overlooking the city centre, were built between 1957 and 1966. Harking back to Le Corbusier's 1930 project Shrapnel for Algiers, and to his even earlier project for Rio de Janiero, the city architects devised a

1 Marshal McLuhan proposes the role of technological front-runner for the creative artist. It is an adaptation of this suggestion which features in architectural circles as Amos Rapoport's theory of the architect as cultural 'pacer'. See Amos Rapoport 'The Personal Element in Housing: an argument for open-ended design' *RIBA Journal* July 1968 (see also p. 90).

serpentine arrangement of blocks ranging in height from four to fourteen storeys, with Le Corbusier's interior motor highways reduced to 10 ft wide open access decks on every third floor. The first occupant at Park Hill was a 'trained social worker' who was detailed to provide feedback to the designers on tenant reaction. The intended social relationships based on the existence of 'streets in the air' failed to materialize – only 4 per cent of the inhabitants 'remembered that (the decks) made it possible to stand and talk to people'[1], while 70 per cent of them complained about the external appearance of the development. Reinforced with this information on the attitudes of the people for whom they were designing, the architects next turned to Hyde Park, the larger of the two developments, and concentrated on taller blocks on the grounds that 'the vertical treatment will con-

(83, 84, 85) High-rise development during the '60s was heavily influenced by the urban imagery of a generation earlier. Le Corbusier's 1930 'Project Shrapnel' for Algiers (83) was the conscious inspiration behind Parkhill and Hyde Park, Sheffield (84, 85), two of the largest and most uncompromising public-sector housing developments ever built in Britain.

site plan, Park Hill
and Hyde Park, Sheffield

key
1. school
2. shops
3. church
4. stadium
5. play area
6. car park

trast with the horizontality of Park Hill to complete the visual composition on the hillside.' The opinions of the occupants of the now completed Hyde Park on this triumph of aesthetic logic have not yet been recorded: unfortunately no resident social worker was laid on this time and the only critical remark the *Review* permitted itself was to note that the 'regularity' of the design had 'produced an undeniable feeling of living in a barracks'.

Personalization

1 N. J. Habraken *De Dragers en de Mensen* Scheltema and Holkema, Amsterdam 1961

It is through recent discussion of the phenomenon of *personalization* (at the mention of which word the city architects of Sheffield no doubt reach for their revolvers), that the weakness of the 'behaviourist' architect in relation to the building user is most clearly seen. N. J. Habraken, the first of many theorists in this field, wrote in 1961:

'Living is an act which takes place in two realms, the public and the private . . . Living exclusively in the public realm is tantamount to institutionalization. Living exclusively in the private realm is a kind of exile. The dwelling must therefore straddle both spheres. In previous centuries an individual built his own home within the public realm; but in doing so established his private realm also. A public authority which builds houses must allow them to be completed in the private realm, otherwise the . . . occupant abdicates responsibility for his dwelling.'[1]

He added prophetically that the alienated modern urban dweller tended to '*undergo*' his town and find 'self expression more in keeping with his nomadic life [driven from place to place by the cycle of development/decay/redevelopment] in his motorcar'. Habraken himself concluded that the only way out of this impasse was for the dwelling to be divorced from its support structure in the same way as the automobile is divorced from the road: an idea which was adopted by others in the 1960s.

Some however did not despair of the traditional but sought inspiration amongst the 'noble savages' of the private-sector housing estates where, beyond reach of the benevolent dictatorship of the public sector, and shielded by social class from the freezing gaze of the architect-Savonarola, they tried to prove that ancient traditions had painlessly adapted themselves to automobiles, television and popular culture in general.

Even as the earnest sociologist sketched furniture layouts in some public sector barracks, so did eager observers of a new and modest type patrol *culs de sac* and avenues in search of 'personalization'. Speedily the most marvellous variety was found in rows of semi-detached dwellings whose very monotony had been criticized a few years before. Sunburst gates, concrete gnomes, window boxes, multi-coloured curtains, picket fences, carriage lanterns, car ports, crazy paving and all the minutiae of external decoration suddenly assumed the status of portents in an unfamiliar world. Facts about the growth of the 'Do it Yourself' business were speedily welded to an idea of territoriality culled (once again) from animal physiology, and the whole put forward as final proof of the heroic struggle of the unsung suburbanite against the grey forces of uniformity and dehumanization. Mock Tudor was rehabilitated and doubtless research is currently in progress to discover some hitherto ignored exponent of the genre suitable for canonization. Any architect appearing at his office in doublet and hose, far from being the subject of ridicule, would today be earnestly questioned and probably emulated.

The polemical advantages of this posture proved legion. For a start there could now be little doubt that the very existence of the public sector, with its anonymity, rat-in-maze experiments, barrack-like structures and infinite graduations of restriction on self expression was an affront to human dignity. With exponentially increasing modesty the new 'libertarian' school sawed away at the arrogance of their 'behaviourist' colleagues. Like rampaging students publishing the contents of secret CIA files they dragged the paraphernalia of 'tight-fit functionalism' out for all to see. Amos Rapoport wrote as follows about the magazine-featured public-sector housing projects of the last ten years:

'The designs generally have fewer elements that can be personalized, show less opportunity for change – fewer surfaces which can be repainted; fewer forms which can be modified; fewer parts which can be changed – than in the average spec-built house . . . Often there are no spare bedrooms for visitors, and where they exist they are not large enough for other activities. One living space is often provided for all activities, so that different leisure activities cannot go on simultaneously, and there is no room for equipment, clothes, books and hobbies. Kitchens are too small to accommodate new and larger appliances as they become available and accepted.'[1]

Further along the same track, but with less emphasis on 'self expression' and more still on consumer durables, Cowburn[2] notes that: 'People want a standardized article which they can "own", "embrace" and "understand". [They] can "embrace" the car, the fridge and the detached bungalow, not the insignificant unit in a block of flats!' As for durables, the home should be designed to display 'cars, caravans or motorboats', a manifest impossibility in high density and high-rise projects where in any case opportunities for personalization of any kind are drastically reduced. The 'rejection of functionalism as a design method', concludes Cowburn, is a 'fairly basic human urge, apparent all over the world'. Noble was quoted earlier on the responsibilities of the 'social engineer' ('the success or failure of our work may depend on our ability to predict human behaviour'). If his words are still to be taken seriously we can only assume that his prediction of 'human behaviour' in the high-rise public sector dwelling consisted largely of walking home from work, eating fish fingers in the living room and going to bed.

The conflict which now exists between the public sector 'behaviourists' and the private sector 'libertarians' is by no means as unequal as it might appear. An enormous accumulation of administrative power, as well as the considerable capital value of its completed dwellings, buttresses the public-sector monolith, and those architects either directly employed in it or largely dependent on it for commissions are unlikely to voluntarily relinquish their position. At the same time the status of the 'libertarian' architect is dubious. Having rejected art to espouse functionalism, itself in turn rejected by science as a result of the inadequacy of the 'behaviourist' atrocities of the scientistic school, there is nowhere else to go but down. By adopting marketing techniques – the course advocated

by 'libertarians' – the architect will voluntarily retreat into the second rank: neither art nor science but commerce. Cowburn himself sees a particularly modest future as 'a professional agent for people who are not able to carry out the appropriate functions themselves'.[3] But it is doubtful if all 'libertarians' would be so easily satisfied. Rapoport, in particular, still seems to cling to the rather élitist idea that the architect might operate as a 'pacemaker' for popular culture – weaning the masses over to good taste by easy stages.[4]

The trick really will be to combine existing economic power – attested to by the volume and cost of advertising to the architectural profession – with a genuine desire to encourage the 'mass client' to develop his individual creativity. If the architect's office is to become a sort of 'citizens advice bureau of the environment', if the public sector is to be dismembered, architectural research to concentrate on motivational analysis and market research of the kind used in the motor industry, and housing welfare to concentrate on the provision of subsidized purchase in the free market, then considerable economic and political changes will be necessary. Further freeing of initiative is already spoken of in libertarian circles[5] – for example, the rescinding of zoning legislation, increased use of marginal agricultural land for housing, rewriting of public health regulations around anti-biotics, reduction of architecture to 'enclosure' and abandonment of all 'monumental values'. Such changes would in turn involve considerable political change – amounting to a revolution in environmental legislation. Yet the authors of such ideas are architects, planners and geographers – politically supine to a man. The idea that such a drastic reversal of planning and housing policy could be carried through without the vigorous support of one or other of the major political parties is at present unthinkable – so at present the 'behaviourists' hold the economic and political centre. In all probability the careers of the 'libertarians' will follow a course depressingly familiar in political if not architectural history. Acting as propagandists for a new world they will lack the courage to seize it when occasion serves and the initiative will pass to an even more extreme party.

1 Amos Rapoport 'The Personal Element in Housing: an argument for open-ended design' RIBA Journal, July 1968

2 William Cowburn 'Popular Housing' Arena The Journal of the Architectural Association. October 1966

3 W. Cowburn 'Popular Housing' op. cit.

4 A. Rapoport 'The Personal Element in Housing' RIBA Journal July 1968, see f.n. p. 85.

5 These are listed in 'non-plan' (New Society, March 21st 1969), an article written jointly by Reyner Banham, Peter Hall, Paul Barker and Cedric Price.

(86) Percy Jenkins threatens suicide in an attempt to prevent the authorities compulsorily purchasing his home as part of a London redevelopment project.

98

7 No exit

'Percy Jenkins made a last defiant bid to save his home yesterday . . . but failed. For four hours he resisted bailiffs and police, council officials and welfare workers. He roared at them from the roof top, threatened to hurl himself from a 30 ft high window ledge and barricaded his doors. But in the end, weeping he had to concede defeat.'

Daily Mirror London 19 June 1969

Private-sector building

In Britain the abandonment of building licensing in 1954 heralded the beginning of a dramatic growth in the dominant private-sector financing organization – the Building Society. Linked indissolubly to the concept of home ownership, and thus to the fortunes of marketing enthusiasts, the rapid growth of these non-profit making societies throughout the period covered by this book, exemplifies both the strength and the weakness of an untrammelled private sector.

From 1430 until the Rationalizing Acts of 1832, 1867 and 1884, the right to vote in Britain – in the county court and later the government – was dependent on the ownership of land to the value of forty shillings. Among the means employed to overcome this drastic restriction of the franchise was the Freehold Land Society, an organization with its roots in the eighteenth century when many such societies existed for the purpose of collecting by monthly subscription sufficient money to purchase forty-shilling plots. The oldest accredited society was founded in 1781 in Birmingham, but it is known that the practice originated long before that date. Although for franchise purposes it was unnecessary to build upon the land purchased, the practice of doing so became increasingly common so that the societies began to change their nature,

advancing money for building and purchase as they do today. This new role was recognized officially by the Building Societies Act of 1836, by which time the franchise regulations had been changed and the original purpose of the societies was fast disappearing.

By 1872 some 2000 societies existed, having between them advanced approximately £17 million for house and land purchase. After World War I the number of societies dropped by half but annual advances had risen to £124,215 million by 1934. By that time the perpetuation of rent restrictions had made the advantages of ownership over rental clearer and after World War II growth began in earnest. By 1967 annual advances had reached £1·5 billion and the average annual rate of growth for all societies since 1960 had been 14 per cent. In the same year building societies lent £11·25 million to the Greater London Council for re-lending to borrowers who could not themselves meet society loan conditions. In 1968 it was confidently announced that the total resources of the building society movement amounted to 70 per cent of those of the London clearing banks. By 1971 total assets of £11 billion are expected.

Ten years earlier the evident capacity of an

1 A full discussion of the performance of the private sector in British house building since the nineteenth century is given in *The Cost of Council Housing* by Hamish Gray, Institute of Economic Affairs, London 1968. Gray concludes that the private sector can provide dwellings faster and cheaper than the public sector, also that the overall correlation between total and private house building (+0·75) is considerably stronger than that between total and public house building (+0·34)

unshackled private sector to shoulder a major part of the housing burden[1] had already led to attacks on the expensive and rigidly structured public-housing system. Denied reduced rates of interest (not to be granted until 1967) the local authority housing subsidy, added to that of the government, rose to £104 million in 1954 and was continuing to rise at the annual rate of 10 per cent. As in the 1930s the government responded by curtailing public-sector building, restricting it to slum clearance and the construction of old people's accommodation. They went further: rent restrictions were cancelled in 1957 and the sale of council houses to their tenants was encouraged. By 1958 public-sector completions were half those of 1954 – a mere 130,000 dwellings. With the two major elements of 1919 housing policy – local-authority housing and rent restriction – severely weakened, the private sector began its dramatic rise to a peak near quarter of a million completions in 1964. Four years later it was estimated that nearly 50 per cent of all separate dwellings in Britain were owner-occupied.

However, inflation continued to exact a price for this phenomenal growth. The money building societies advance has first to be collected from savers, many of whom turned away from the societies towards the unit trusts which after 1964 were offering higher interest rates. As a consequence the societies themselves offered higher dividends, raising their own interest rates to maintain liquidity and raising the average monthly repayment on an 80 per cent mortgage from £18 to £30 between 1966 and 1969.

Owing to prices and incomes restrictions over the 1967–9 period, earnings failed to keep up with this increase in monthly payments and the parallel rise in the price of houses themselves. Giving up hope of house purchase under these terms many resorted to the local-authority lists which in consequence lengthened dramatically. The building societies, hypnotized by their boasts of 1968, began to consider desperate expedients such as forty-year mortgages. The repayments thus entailed would total over three and a half times the original advance.

(87, 88) The process of rationalization which has characterized the building industry since the end of wartime austerity has also extended to the design and layout of housing developments, particularly since the adoption of Parker Morris space standards by the public sector. The two estates here are contemporaneous, dating from the mid-'60s. Similarities in layout and design are obvious but the private-sector estate (87) is sited amongst woods in a suburb, whilst the more densely planned public-sector estate occupies an infill site next to a railway (88).

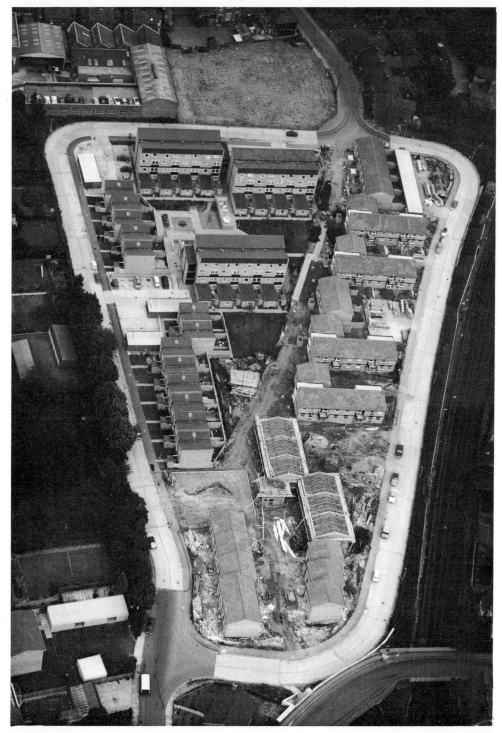

In one particular sector of the market the building societies had already begun to lend over comparatively long periods. The voluntary housing movement, begun by Owen, Cadbury and Lever in the nineteenth century but since overshadowed by the massive development of public housing, gained renewed support in 1964 with the establishment of the Housing Corporation. This organization, funded with a government grant, was intended to provide one-third of the construction cost of approved voluntary housing schemes and enabled housing societies to borrow the remainder from building societies over a period of forty years. Under this arrangement projects for 3300 units were approved in 1965, 5600 in 1966, and 10,500 in 1967. The modest target for this growth was an output of 20,000 units a year by 1972. Unfortunately, the rapid rise in interest rates which began in 1968 cut severely into this performance and by 1969 the Corporation was obliged to use all its allocation to finance the completion of approved schemes for which mortgages could not be found.

One very important reason for the increased popularity of house purchase by long-term mortgage, has been the steady inflation of house prices which, since the middle fifties, has compensated for, and even exceeded, the rising cost of purchasing finance. This steadily increasing market value is also a disappointingly simple explanation for the popularity of 'do it yourself' personalization in the private sector. Far from every car port, sun loggia and extra-roomed loft representing a monument to the indomitable struggle of the suburban dweller against standardization, such developments often represent nothing more than a further investment in the increasing value of the house to which they are attached.

Today, because housing has been a sellers' market for as long as most people can remember, the spiral of prices and interest rates may have unwittingly reached a socially critical level. Nearly 50 per cent of the 18 million dwellings in Britain are owner-occupied, and income distribution among the population is such that a high proportion of these not only carry mortgages but are owned by individuals who for some years have taken increased rates as *an addition to the sum they owe* – rather than in the form of increased payments. As a result their mortgages will tend to run on well beyond the twenty to twenty-five years originally envisaged, deep into retirement age when income is drastically reduced.

The result of steadily increasing subsidies to keep pace with inflation – particularly if incomes fail to rise in proportion – could be the establishment of a colossal edifice of relative repayment rates bearing little or no resemblance to the original conception of home ownership. Under these conditions the transfer of credit obligations from owner to owner, or from father to son, would clearly be more logical than buying or selling a house. In this way the owner-occupier market in Britain might easily come to resemble that of Switzerland, where house purchase credit is often taken out for an indefinite period (on payment of interest) and thereafter transferred from owner to owner. In any case, the unilateral subsidy of an unopposed private sector, because of the need for loans and subsidies on an enormous scale, would inevitably create circumstances analogous to those of an unopposed public sector. Either way state intervention and manipulation of the market is inevitable.

Winner loses

It is just over fifty years since the government first took a serious hand in the problem of housing the people of this country. During this time the population has risen by approximately 16 million and the number of dwellings by over 9 million, so that while the population has only increased by one-third, the number of dwellings in the country has doubled. On the face of it this looks like a not inconsiderable improvement, an impression reinforced by further statistics which indicate that the number of persons per dwelling has fallen from 4·7 in 1921 to 3·1 in 1961 and is probably significantly under 3 today. In the same vein it can be noted that whereas 90 per cent of the 9 million-odd dwellings in existence in 1914 were rented from wicked private landlords, today half the 17 million dwellings in the country are owned by the people who live in them; a further 27 per cent belong to local authorities and only 23 per cent are still owned and rented by private landlords. Better yet, 57 per cent of those in the privately rented sector – which today comprises both the most luxurious and the most poverty stricken accommodation – have their rents controlled and are thus safe from arbitrary increases. Similarly the extent of the legal protection afforded a tenant against eviction today is unexampled in history. Eighty-eight per cent of the dwellings in the United Kingdom are either owned outright by their occupants, in the process of purchase by mortgage through a Building Society, publicly owned and rented at a considerable subsidy by a local authority, or protected from the vagaries of the accommodation market by rent controls and legal guarantees of tenure. This amounts to a complete reversal of the situation at the outbreak of World War I. If we add to this tale of success the by now famous – or infamous – prediction of a surplus of a million houses by 1973, the case for regarding public intervention in the housing market as a triumph seems unanswerable. Unfortunately there is another side to the picture.

Of the 17 million dwellings now in existence, 2 million are slums classified as unfit for human habitation, being defective in terms of repair, stability, freedom from damp, natural lighting, ventilation, water supply, drainage or storage space or any combination of these factors. A further 2 million houses are in an unsatisfactory condition lacking one or more of five basic amenities. In addition to the high proportion of slum or marginal property – itself a reflection of the relatively high proportion of British housing built before World War I – there is the problem of overcrowding and the disaster of homelessness. Approximately 400,000 families were living in overcrowded conditions in 1967 while 3000 families were in hostels for the homeless following eviction from accommodation, mostly privately rented. Waiting lists for council accommodation have lengthened dramatically in recent years with those in the GLC area heading the tables with an increase from 150,000 families in 1965 to over a quarter of a million in 1970. Comparable increases have been registered in Birmingham, Glasgow and Liverpool and an even more ominous statistic emerged from a Lambeth survey which indicated that only 14 per cent of those eligible for council accommodation had in fact put their names on the list.

Rising standards and, more importantly, rising expectations, have made the situation of the urban poor intolerable. The phrase urban poor is used advisedly in this context for an important aspect of the housing problem is its urban nature. 80 per cent of the population of Britain are urban dwellers, 27 per cent of them living in the London conurbation alone. This largely urban population includes about 500,000 families living on incomes lower than the rate payable by the Ministry of Social Security in order to ensure 'the maintenance of civilized standards'.

Such statistics as these are relatively well

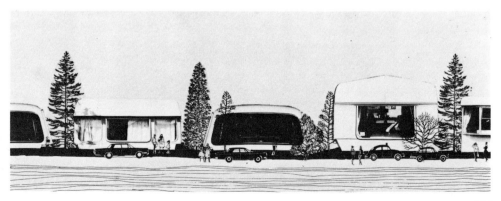

(89) William Cowburn's montage of caravans as consumer housing in a suburban setting. This image of the territorial past of land ownership *allied* to the evolving concept of mobility represents a prolongation of the earliest ideas about industrialized building. The caravan versus house arguments would certainly seem to justify some such compromise but there is no tendency in this direction to be discerned within the sub-culture most attuned to movement.

known. They indicate that despite considerable efforts by public and private sector alike a great deal remains to be done before the people of Britain can be properly housed. What they do not show is that the whole mechanism for providing finance, subsidies and targets which has operated – with interruptions – for the last fifty years is in grave danger of overturning from the accumulated weight of its own reliance upon a market economy kept alive by a variety of expedients, each more extreme and dangerous than the last. Housing finance today is like a bizarre tropical plant which can only be kept alive under carefully controlled conditions. It is watched through glass screens by

(90) The contrast between the two modes in which housing problems are discussed is expressed by this fine piece of civic sculpture (protected against vandals by wire), presiding over the demolition of an earlier pattern of settlement. The resemblance of the process of demolition to the destruction of the *evidence* of earlier ways of life has not escaped exponents of territoriality and personalization in housing.

experts so specialized that they are unable to imagine any alternative species. They keep alive a plant whose whole historical context and purpose is gone, and all the time the temperature outside the glass case is falling and their task grows more difficult. In the public sector the cost of maintenance rises to equal the cost of loan servicing

and thus eventually cuts down the number of units which can be built. In the sphere of the housing societies, as we have seen, crippling interest rates drastically reduce the number of projects which can be financed according to the one-third government, two-thirds building society principle. In the owner-occupier market the cost of an average mortgage has risen by 25 per cent in five years and the average industrial weekly wage is now one-third lower than that same average mortgage repayment. *The number of people who earn enough to buy a house has been halved since 1964 by the rise in interest rates and by the side effects of inflation.*

These are warning signs and their causes lie deep in the nature of housing policy and finance. With an effective housing policy producing 500,000 dwellings per year, a marginal increase in real income and interest rates pegged at around the 6 per cent mark, the problems of homelessness, rehabilitation, slum clearance and local authority waiting lists could be tackled with some hope of progress – under present conditions there is no such hope: housing has gone into reverse.

The figures may seem stark yet they greatly obscure the human suffering which the housing crisis supports. The sole national voice for these otherwise defenceless victims is the popular press. Here in a thousand tales of administrative incompetence and cruelty is to be found the other side of the problem – the real tragedy of housing policy. Barbed wire surrounds council flats, bailiffs and detectives plot to gain entry, squatters fight with Mayor and Councillors, old age pensioners cling to cottages isolated by the rubble of demolition, 'spokesmen for the council' make appalling remarks, pickets surround hostels for the homeless where families may not stay together, farm cottages are torched in error, industrially built high-rise flats suffer inexplicable progressive collapse, an old lady is served her third successive compulsory purchase order in three successive houses in ten years, families are discovered in subsidized council accommodation 'living it up' on combined incomes of over £80 per week, deranged demolition men dynamite their homes when threatened with eviction,

(91) The semi-detached council house which a father of seven blew to pieces with gelignite after a dispute over rent arrears. The incident, which occurred in Oxford in June 1969, was widely reported in the national and local press but ignored by 'behaviourist' students of the activities of local-authority tenants: presumably it was thought less interesting than the disposition of furniture in the dwelling immediately prior to the explosion.

men who 'resisted Hitler's bombers' are hustled out of their own houses by 'police and bailiffs, housing officials, welfare workers and a doctor', village mums lie in the path of traffic, walls peel and ceilings sag, homelessness increases, twenty people still share a single lavatory and little children look out from grainy photographs with expressions no one can be paid to make.[1]

This is the tactile end of the graphs and figures and efforts that adorn the walls of the professionals. The sociological/statistical jargon in which housing is discussed at the official level has no analogue at the level of purchase or tenancy, where terminology reminiscent of shipwreck, goldstrike or natural disaster is common. This shocking contrast, an earnest of the strength of the emotions lying submerged beneath the jargon, rarely surfaces at the official level save under the pressure of some catastrophe such as Ronan Point, or the trauma associated with eviction or large rent or rates increases, yet its presence is undeniable. The middle-aged council tenants of Birmingham, whose tenure

was in any case secure for the duration of their lives, repeatedly used phrases like 'waiting all our lives . . . a lifelong desire . . . our last chance . . . almost too late', to describe the purchase of the freehold to properties they had in some cases occupied for as long as twenty years.[2]

Writing of the crucial importance of morale in the survival of victims of shipwreck Alain Bombard noted that death often occurred after three days, before food or water was exhausted and in the absence of intolerable weather conditions. This he attributed to the fact that 'when his ship goes down a man's whole universe goes with it. Because he no longer has a deck under his feet courage and reason abandon him.'[3] This diagnosis corresponds to evidence from anthropology, animal physiology and psychology. Lévi-Strauss records that the South American Borero tribe allowed their culture to disintegrate after missionaries had 'persuaded' them to rearrange the order of the dwellings in their villages to correspond to a gridiron.[4] Similarly the deprivation of personal en-

1 These stories were drawn at random from the files of the London *Daily Mirror*, March 1968 – August 1969

2 Conservative Party Political Broadcast on the sale of council houses to tenants. March 1967

3 Alain Bombard. *Naufrage Volontaire* Editions de Paris 1953

4 Claude Lévi-Strauss. *The Savage Mind.* Weidenfeld & Nicolson 1966

vironment, including clothing, which is often a concomittant of admission to hospitals, prisons or asylums for the insane, can have comparable effects to those described by Bombard. A crisis of identity occurs whose pathology has been well documented by such shrewd observers as Laing,[1] Goffman[2] and Searles.[3]

From the popular press reports mentioned above, the interviews with council house purchasers, and the success of such emotionally based fund raising campaigns as that operated by Shelter,[4] it seems perfectly credible that the loss of a house is equivalent to shipwreck, and the non-possession of a house equivalent to swimming for your life. In this case the Industrial Revolution, the population explosion and the dawn of affluence may well have intensified rather than diminished the territorial significance of the home: its importance today transcends what we tend to regard as its fundamental purpose, that of shelter, and moves into the vital area of individual identity. A person without a home is like a traveller who has lost his passport, foreign currency and credit cards: he has no evidence to prove that he is who he says he is – his very existence (in official terms) is in doubt. Thus we have no alternative but to regard fifty years housing effort as a failure: we are not clearing slums fast enough, we are not building houses fast or cheaply enough, and we have grave doubts about the suitability of much of what we do construct.

1 R. D. Laing. *The Divided Self*. Penguin Books, London 1965

2 Erving Goffman. *Essays on the Social Situation of Mental Patients and other Inmates*.

3 Harold Searles. *The Nonhuman Environment* IUP. New York 1960

4 SHELTER, an organization formed in December 1966, has been very successful in raising money for the homeless – largely as a result of a very particularised and emotional approach. After raising £1,000,000 in two years of operation SHELTER has gone into housing itself with community redevelopment projects in several large cities including London and Liverpool.

(92, 93) Proceeding from the *pilotis* on which Le Corbusier erected many of his most famous projects, the modern movement tended in one sense toward the levitation of the building from the landscape. The houses by Richard Neutra, at Sherman Oaks, California (92), illustrate the process of liberation which led to the caravan and the truly mobile home (93). The tendency towards mobile structures derives to some extent from the cost advantage accruing to products clearly separated from the legal pitfalls of land ownership. The motor car which enjoyed just such separation from the cost and complexity of road building illustrates this process at its most successful.

8 New directions

'I like to think
    (right now please!)
of a cybernetic forest filled with pines
and electronica where deer stroll peacefully
past computers as if they were flowers
with spinning blossoms.'

The Realist (Quoted by David Greene
Architectural Design May 1969)

Faced with this situation the response of the architectural profession has been both evasive and utopian. Persisting with the *première moderne* separation of building from land, most theorists have ignored the shattering legal and political implications of such a step taken to its logical conclusion. At the same time the dancing image of the automobile – the great technological success of the twentieth century – has come to mean much more than the vindication of machine production it represented to the pre-war pioneers. Even so, its full implications are for the most part ignored.

Not merely a means of transport, but an extension of individual personality and mobility, the car has more in common with a suit of clothes than with a bus or a train. Driving is not the same as being carried, just as taking photographs is not the same as merely looking. In many ways the therapy of movement associated with driving (particularly in Europe where car design and road conditions stress manual as opposed to automatic control) explains more about the overwhelming popular success of the car than do objective studies of traffic movement or analyses of the economics of car ownership.[1] Motor vehicles have emerged as anti-planning weapons and no amount of computerized traffic control, parking restriction, performance limitation, credit curtailment or road pricing is likely to change fundamentally the use to which they are put.

Of course the problems presented by the automobile as part of a movement system are exactly equalled by the enormous potential for freedom conferred by the vehicle itself. That is the uneasy stasis which balances mobility and stability today. But just as

1 See Stephen Black
Man and Motorcars
Secker and Warburg,
London 1964

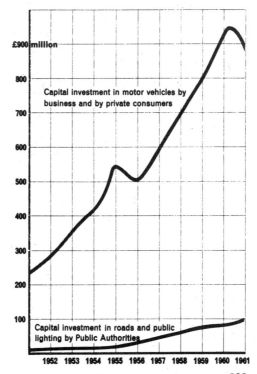

£900 million

Capital investment in motor vehicles by business and by private consumers

800

700

600

500

400

300

200

100

Capital investment in roads and public lighting by Public Authorities

1952 1953 1954 1955 1956 1957 1958 1959 1960 1961

(94) This graph shows the enormous disparity between the sums spent on cars and on roads in Britain. A similar graph matching land costs in relation to housing would show a similarly disproportionate emphasis on land.

1 R. B. White
'Prefabrication – past,
present and potential'
RIBA Journal, September
1962 (author's italics)

2 N. J. Habraken *De
Dragers en de Mensen*
Scheltema and Holkema,
Amsterdam 1961

emphasis on personal movement separates the idea of the car from that of the house, so does simultaneous consideration of the two alien conditions adumbrate a kind of synthesis of the two, the caravan, which did indeed come into widespread use before 1940. During the post-war period, development of mobile or semi-mobile living using this hybrid form was particularly rapid in the United States, where by 1961 trailer homes accounted for thirteen per cent of all dwellings sold.

In Europe, however, higher population densities and a general absence of virgin land allied to restrictive legislation, conspired to retard the growth of mobile home ownership by reinforcing the economic advantages of traditional housing. Writing in 1962, R. B. White noted:

'A caravan, which is a fully prefabricated, movable unit of accommodation, will provide one small room of about 1000 cubic ft volume, having a useful life of perhaps twenty years, at a cost of say £800. For about twice that sum it is possible to build a fixed abode of ten times that cubic capacity with a useful life of at least sixty years, and which, compared with the short-term product, will certainly require less maintenance. The cost of financing the fixed abode will be less, particularly if the factory product is bought on hire purchase . . . *moreover, the house is tied to a piece of land whose value will tend to appreciate.*'[1]

The last sentence sums up the market strength of traditional owner-occupied housing; it also reveals the main defect in the process of redevelopment, which, until recently, was the cornerstone of housing policy. The subsidized construction of large numbers of houses – even when segregated into rival privately-owned and publicly-rented estates, as in Britain – has the effect of increasing land value through scarcity, particularly when zoning and density restric-tions prevent untrammelled expansion of the kind practised between the wars. This would not be the case provided sufficient houses could be built to guarantee a surplus in all major population areas – but this cannot be done simply because urban areas by their very nature generate land values so high that the cost of constructing anything other than luxury dwellings (as well as the legal complexities and delays resulting from compulsory purchase) became prohibitive. Even when ambitious plans to rehouse the occupants of congested urban areas are forced through, the density and public health regulations now in force ensure that fewer people are re-housed than were dispossessed. Thus redevelopment steadily undermines its own programme, and tends to prolong the state of emergency which brought it into being.[2]

If the dwelling could really be separated from land ownership or tenancy, the problems of redevelopment would assume a new and more manageable guise resembling that pertaining to the disposal and replacement of automobiles. When one buys a car one does not have at the same time to purchase a stretch of road. Neither does one have directly to pay for road construction or maintenance. Until recently even parking was free and the disposal of unwanted vehicles – though still a problem – cannot be compared to the agonies of demolition and clearance inseparable from the process of urban renewal. The car is practically free while its wheels are turning – its problems begin when they stop. It is only when *immobile,* in a traffic jam or parked, that the difficulties of car ownership and distribution begin to assume the intractability of those normally associated with housing and the built environment. The deduction is obvious: split housing from land and it could become cheap – attach cars to roads and they become not merely expensive, but immersed in the legal and administrative jungle which surrounds permanent structure.

Housing as a total system

'It is a well-known argument in the capitalist world that you have to have competition for things to improve. That is not correct because the telephone was a complete monopoly from the beginning. They didn't sell the telephone, they sold a service, and they found that every time they improved the telephone more people used it: they saw that it paid them to go on increasing the distances it could operate over and generally improving the service. Without you asking for it they continually replaced your telephone with a better one. Now if they had *sold* those early telephones there would have been a Christopher Wren telephone, a Louis XIV telephone . . . in World War One there would have been a Trench type telephone . . . all this horrible equipment you would have paid a fantastic price for would have stopped development of the service itself. The lesson of the telephone taught me back in 1927 that housing was going to have to be a service industry.'
Richard Buckminster Fuller 1970

As the above quotation indicates, the idea of bringing the mountain to Mohammed in terms of a solution to the housing problem has a genealogy of some forty years already. The image of the house as a kind of telephone can now take its place alongside the traditional castle and the modern machine for living in as a generic concept, designed to fire the imagination of contemporary and future housing theorists. Using this new image the thorny age-old problem can now be seen in a new light: instead of designing houses, manipulating subsidies or fighting to keep a balance between inflationary value and inflationary cost, today's housing theorist should be engaged in designing a *housing system*. He should be working towards a situation where – to speak metaphorically – the old housing machine gun, hosing its target with perhaps 300,000 completed houses a year, becomes transformed into an internal combustion engine which *contains* all the little explosions of construction and feeds part of the energy generated by them back into the process of maintenance, so that a

steady, continuous process of housing provision, use, obsolescence and modernization – a completed circle in fact – replaces the present disconnected pattern of construction, decay and new construction.

This process would require a splitting down of the housing unit into basic elements for manufacture, finance and maintenance – an idea which has been developed both theoretically and practically in recent years by N. J. Habraken, Director of the *Stichting Architecten Research* (SAR) in the Netherlands. Habraken has set in train a considerable programme of research and practical work which recently culminated in the decision of the Netherlands government to authorize the construction of a new town at Maarssen Broeck – situated between Amsterdam and Utrecht – where a population of 40,000 will be housed in dwellings conceived as binary structures in the form support frame plus detachable units. Habraken explains the theoretical background to this development as follows:

'The industrialization of housing which is so often discussed is nothing but the mechanization of the *mass-housing project* as it has been understood since the turn of the century. If we wish to investigate the conditions necessary for an industrialized *housing process* we must bear in mind that the two things are not at all similar. In order to devise a true *process* we must build dwellings whose interior arrangement as well as exterior form can be removed, replaced, altered or updated independently of its neighbours. Up to now this has only been possible with single-storey detached housing – a fact which may go far to explain the popularity of that type. For our purposes this kind of flexibility must be made available to the high density, high-rise dwelling as well.'

This done, the dwelling unit itself must be continuously modified and renewed, like a car or an airliner, independent of its ground support structure.

111

The vague sense of disappointment that one feels on discovering that Habraken's brilliantly expressed critique of the housing process has led only to a system the employment of which must reduce still further the control the architect can exert over the *form* of mass housing, may be merely a facet of the withdrawal symptoms experienced by many architects over the loss of a formerly assumed omnipotence. It is curious that the very people who in Britain deplore NBA standard house plans, yardstick control of housing costs and impending 'rules for environment' from the Ministry of Housing, are often most impressed by Habraken's attacks on current housing practice – imagining as they do that they are the precursors of astonishing new perspectives for the architect. They are not. Instead Habraken's binary structure offers new perspectives for the building user. All the advantages under the SAR system accrue to the occupier who within reasonable limits can not only design his own dwelling but adapt and modify it with ease, so that the estimated ten-year life of components facilitates rather than diminishes opportunities for change.

For Habraken the establishment of stable environmental areas by means of support structures, coupled with the facilitation of internal change by means of detachable units, answers the question of the architect's involvement in 'personalization', 'territoriality', 'image building' or any other *recherché* remnant of architectural omnipotence. The very simplicity and duplicatibility of the solution explains his 'fatalism' about its eventual adoption. The traditional methodology of mass housing, less capable of coming to terms with increases in the size, range and capability of consumer durables than the spacious urban housing of the eighteenth century, possesses no advantage at all over what Habraken proposes. As he says, attempts to industrialize the mass-housing project resemble attempts to 'manufacture the seventeenth-century coach by means of an industrial production system'. The fundamental separation between dwelling unit and support structure represents for the first time a correct analogy with the methods of production used in the automobile industry. For the first time the house is to be financially and structurally separated from its land support, as the car has always been separated from the road. The precise details of the system employed are of little importance; the support structure can range from simple party walls with concrete floor slabs to a triangulated megastructure. The important thing is the separation. At the same time, to take the automobile analogy further, the rental or hire-purchase of detachable units, together with the usual consumer durables, may undermine the principle of ownership altogether – continuing the process whereby hiring and credit sale are replacing the traditional idea of possession with a new one of *temporary rights over things*.

Promising as this process sounds, it is necessary to offer a word of caution. Even assuming that it would be comparatively easy to introduce a *structural* and *financial separation* of the kind developed by Habraken into both sectors of the housing market in Britain, the results of so doing would be merely palliative for many years to come. We add only about two per cent to our stock of housing annually, and the gradual introduction of more flexible housing systems could not seriously effect the operational life of the remainder for at least a quarter of a century. Only a change in life style – followed or led by rationalizing legislation – can bring about a *radical* alteration in the gloomy housing prospect facing the Western nations.

It is here that the general failure of architectural theory to connect with economic and social realities can be seen at its most serious level: from the 'behaviourist' wing of the profession to the 'libertarians', there is nowhere to be found the utter rejection of the whole complex of land ownership, steady inflation, and declining standards of construction which is a prerequisite of any radical approach to the problem described on previous pages.

Technological superhumanism

Only one group of architects and students in the last decade has come within striking distance of the massive change in life-style so evident in the activities of the young today. This group, which I shall term the technological superhumanist school, has a kind of absolute faith in technology as the 'natural' tool of Western man. In concrete terms, the cardinal design concepts of technological superhumanism are mainly drawn from the spin-off from the 1940–6 transportable and factory-made housing boom. When *Archigram* – a leading superhumanist group – came to construct a genealogy for itself, it selected the '40s, and illustrated numerous artefacts from that period of transient optimism which succeeded World War II. It would, however, be a great error to write off the whole movement as the acts of the sons of the pioneers. Though barely separated by one generation from the pioneer 'prefab' builders, the technological superhumanists incorporate one element into their thinking which, to their forebears, would seem entirely out of context – that of *movement*. Earlier enthusiasts saw the mobility of prefabs as a means to an end: the facilitation of war production, the speeding up of otherwise time-consuming site work, or the provision of housing in undeveloped areas. The technological superhumanists see mobility as an end in itself. In this sense they are completely differentiated from their predecessors. What they propose puts them within range of the growing Hippie subculture, whose transient gatherings and itinerant life-style became more clearly defined towards the close of the '60s. If we assume, for a moment, this connection between technological superhumanism and the youth movement in the West, we begin to see how unique their position is. Superhumanism draws its evidence – and its *de facto* support – from a social group well removed from the *traditional* centres of power and influence, but close to the *emergent* power groups both in business – through pop – and in politics – through revolution. The connection is to be sure *de facto* rather than *de jure*, but there are no alternative possibilities. Architecture of the official, institutional mode – the province of the be-haviourists – is irretrievably compromised in the eyes of the young; architecture as advocated by the libertarians is politically reactionary and by definition a distinctly middle-class affair. If any architectural theory is to connect at all it must be that of the technological superhumanists who have extended the idea of removing the building from the land by *pilotis* to a level of impermanence and mobility undreamed of by any first-generation pioneer, with the exception of Richard Buckminster Fuller. Their idea is utterly revolutionary, not only in the context of architectural theory, but in the simple political fact that whoever proposes to disconnect the building from land, for whatever reason, is proposing a violation of one of the fundamental principles of all capitalist economies. Archigram is a revolutionary organization – whether it thinks so or not.

Besides being one of the best-known superhumanist groups (apart from the Japanese Metabolists), Archigram has an interesting story in its own right. Starting in 1961 with as unpromising-looking a publication as ever emerged from a student body, Archigram made one or two bold, if elliptical, announcements: 'We want to drag into building some of the poetry of countdown, orbital helmets, discord of mechanical body transportation methods (?) and leg walking'. And: 'WE HAVE CHOSEN TO BYPASS THE DECAYING BAUHAUS IMAGE WHICH IS AN INSULT TO FUNCTIONALISM'. Or, more pointedly as it turned out: 'A new generation of architecture must arise with forms and spaces which seem to reject the precepts of "Modern", yet in fact retain these precepts'.

The first of these statements could be said to have been prophetic; despite the rather solid and 'architectural' look of the schemes illustrated in *Archigram One*, the group did later import NASA ideas wholesale, with the important substitution of dollie birds for androgynous spacemen. The future development of the 'discord of mechanical body transportation methods' is more obscure, while 'leg walking' was shortly to vanish altogether under the influence of TV puppet

(95) The cushicle, designed
by Michael Webb in 1966,
still represents the most
ambitious movement/
enclosure system designed
by Archigram. Intended to
employ an air cushion
instead of wheels, and
inflatable to one more
degree than the *chaise longue*
indicated in the photograph,
the cushicle is based on a
light tubular chassis and
an attachable enclosure.
Webb, who later became
concerned about the asocial
aspects of this project,
redesigned it as the
'suitaloon' two years after.

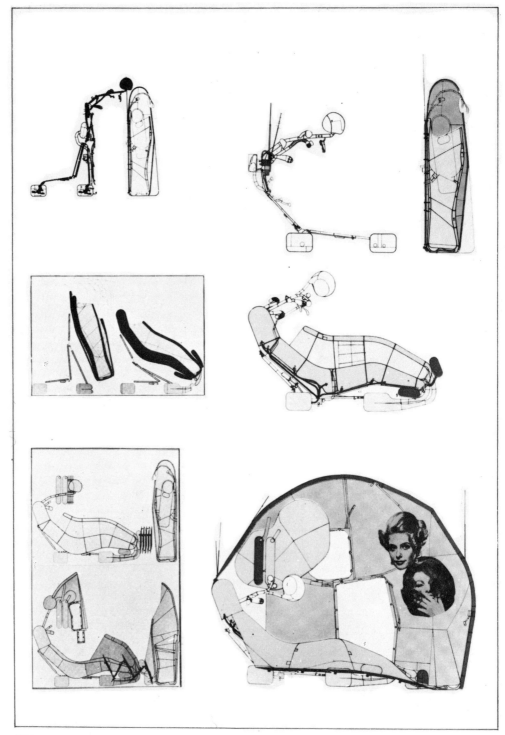

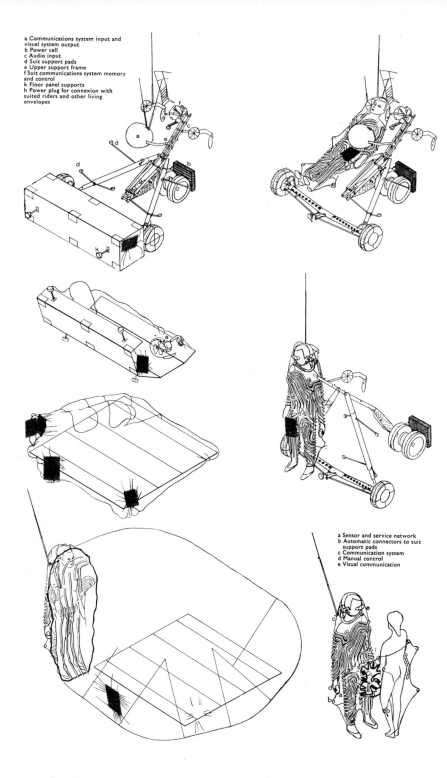

a Communications system input and
  visual system output
b Power cell
c Audio input
d Suit support pads
e Upper support frame
f Suit communications system memory
  and control
k Floor panel supports
h Power plug for connexion with
  suited riders and other living
  envelopes

a Sensor and service network
b Automatic connectors to suit
  support pads
c Communication system
d Manual control
e Visual communication

(96) The suitaloon, 1968.
In this project the cushicle
was both simplified – it
reverted to a tricycle
undercarriage resembling
that of a golf caddy – and
developed into a unit which
could be attached to other
units for social purposes.
The means for achieving
the latter was an increase
in the potential volume of
the inflatable envelope as
well as the incorporation of
means for detaching it
altogether from the vehicle's
chassis. Curiously, the result
of these changes was to
make the vehicle less
convincing as a concept. It
became clear that it would
in the end resemble a sort
of bubblecar with (probably)
a noisy two-stroke engine.

I This breakthrough was no doubt influenced by Reyner Banham's 'Unhouse'; an inflatable, transparent dome carrying a 'standard of living package' powered by a 'beefed-up' car battery. The car itself was used to provide mobility by towing the 'Un-house' in a trailer. This project was first published in *Art in America*, April 1965.

shows. As for the old-style swingeing attack on the Bauhaus, little more was heard of it. Archigram speedily developed a vocabulary of its own, and, after various members of the group had paid visits to California, began to exploit it with great confidence. Unquestionably, one of the key factors in Archigram's success has been their concentration on a non-linear, audiovisual mode of communication, whose impenetrability puzzled the will of old-style literary men, and caused them to hold their fire until it was too late.

Of all the announcements contained in *Archigram One*, the point about a non-modern seeming modernism was unquestionably the most profound. At a distance of ten years, it is plain that the valiant technological superhumanism of Archigram has projected the revolutionary principles of the pioneer modernists further into the future thàn anyone in 1960 could have dared to hope. Eschewing the frustrating determinism of the 'behaviourists', just as they rejected the pseudo-scientific language of their 'experiments', the mad draughtsmen of Archigram outflanked and infiltrated their enemies in all quarters of the globe. When the organizers of Osaka's Expo '70 apprised the official British contributors of their intention to invite Archigram to take part, no British official had ever heard of them.

Of the many Archigram projects, the most relevant to the theme of escape from deter-

minism through movement are undoubtedly the *reductio ad absurdum* of the dwelling carried out by Michael Webb between 1964 and 1969, and the parallel 'Nomad/Instant City' studies. Starting in 1964 with a housing project featuring the automated erection of 400 sq. ft of enclosed living space, Webb anticipated the conclusions reached by Rapoport four years later, by attaching servicing units to the perimeter, so that the actual floor space – though sub-dividable by means of free-forming partitions – remained roughly constant, and the service units could easily be replaced or extended. By 1966, this concept of flexibility had undergone a fundamental change: in 'Drive-in Living', the living area became in part a vehicle and the heavy service units were fixed to a three-dimensional supporting grid. Later still, a major conceptual breakthrough[1] recast the whole enclosure into the form of an inflatable skin which, combined with a tiny hovercraft vehicle called the cushicle, constituted a completely mobile life-support system falling midway between a motor cycle and a tent. The next step, which followed a lengthy visit to America, embodied further refinements including apparently remote sexual contact through the agency of the suitaloon. In this project the suit/envelope has increased flexibility and a less mummified appearance, while the vehicle has retreated from air cushion to tricycle support, developing an uncanny resemblance to a lawnmower in the process. The designer describes the

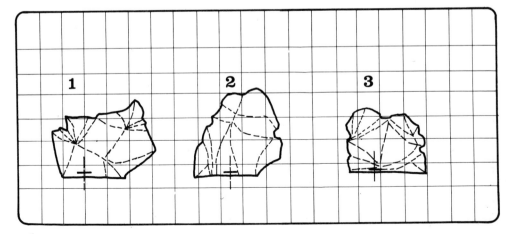

(97, 98) 'The ranges of Logplug and Rokplug shown above are selected GRP simulations of real logs and rocks. They serve to conceal service outlets for semi- or non-autonomous mobile living containers. They would be indistinguishable from the real thing and would thus bring to any setting a high degree of support without detracting from natural beauty' (*Architectural Design* May 1969). Location of camouflaged service outlets was to be by a homing transmitter with a range of one mile.

social potential of this machine-for-living-in thus:

'Each suit has a plug serving a similar function as the key to your front door. You can plug into your friend and you will both be in one envelope, or you can plug into any envelope, stepping out of your suit, the suit being left clipped onto the outside ready to step into when you leave.'[1]

Apart from David Greene's naturally camouflaged rural servicing node ('Can you spot the *rokplugs* and *logplugs*?')[2], Webb's essays into technology of existentialism constitute the most philosophically extreme of all the Archigram projects. On a much larger scale, and far more likely to be realized in a marketable form, is the generic Instant City idea which shares the same 'Nomad' parentage as the cushicle and suitaloon.

1 *Architectural Design* June 1968, p. 272

2 *Ibid* May 1969, p. 275

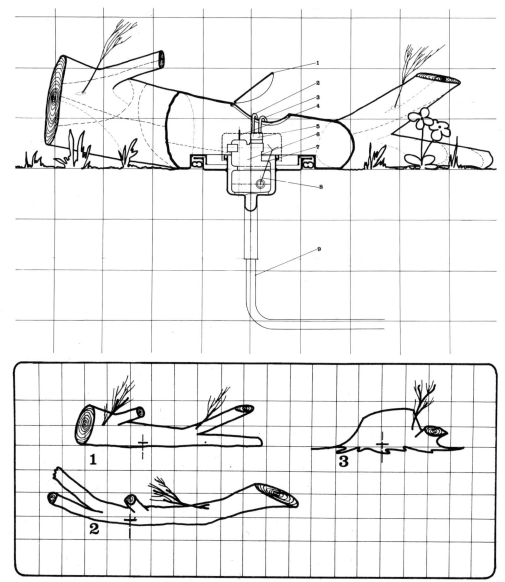

Instant City, as published in 1969, amounted to a mobile media display connected to land lines, incorporating collapsible screens and supporting space frames, inflatable tents and an overall velarium supported by captive balloons. Its announced purpose – to exploit the 'idea of environment as an analog to the collecting together of a multiplicity of factors that can be perceived or experienced' – places it in the mainstream of mechanistic consciousness-simulation; but the semi-political blurb accompanying it ('England in the next half-century must live by its wits or perish') has an entirely novel ring. It is almost as though someone somewhere had told the designers that this one really was going to be built.

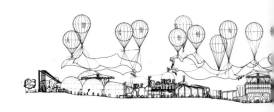

In fact, a major social phenomenon of the very late '60s began to indicate even to the professionally sceptical that Archigram might be on the right track after all. The long-term, multifold trend towards mobility began to assume proportions which made its significance undeniable even to entrenched opponents of the significance of anything done by people under thirty.

Starting in America, open-air pop concerts swiftly spread to Britain. In a semi-literal interpretation of Country Joe's famous remark that his political programme would consist of 'free music in the park', inspired impresarios in London organized a major free concert for the afternoon of 5 July 1969: to their surprise, a quarter of a million people attended. From the 17th to the 19th of the same month, 400,000 people attended the 'Aquarian Exposition of Music and Peace' at Woodstock; another 100,000 allegedly failed to arrive as a result of police roadblocks. Back in Britain, the weekend of 30/31 August saw a repetition of the London formula on the Isle of Wight, in honour of visiting folk-supremo Bob Dylan. This time fewer people attended (an estimated 150,000), press-fabricated tales of sexual licence obscured the scene, and administration was less masterly than on previous occasions. Nonetheless, the longer duration of the spectacle brought forth a remarkable display of temporary dwellings and servicing facilities. Called 'Electronic Inflatable City' by the organizers, this temporary metropolis featured shops, restaur-

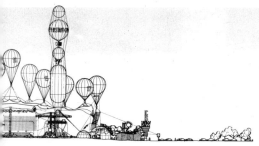

ants, a polystyrene foam bath and other 'indeterminate' installations. The addition of complex servicing and amplification equipment heightened the resemblance of the whole to the contemporary Archigram vision.

This evidence of *connection* with a Western world-wide youth phenomenon is all the more impressive for its isolation. Nowhere else in the theory of architecture *as practised*

(99, 100) Instant City, an Archigram project of 1969, marks the development both of the earlier 'computer city' project and of the general nomadic idea. Here the city has become a kind of mixed-media , information environment which travels from place to place hooking up to media land-lines wherever necessary. The mobile components of the city are comparatively few and light – consisting mainly of tents, balloons and display equipment for the information which is piped from elsewhere. The process of 'McLuhanization' which can be observed here, whereby mechanical *movement* gives way to electronic *configuration*, is perhaps the most advanced aspect of the project.

(101) 'Electronic Inflatable City' on the Isle of Wight, August 1969. The burgeoning success of pop concerts in Britain during 1969 culminated in the Dylan concert where 150,000 people spent the weekend under canvas in the first major approach to the Archigram nomadic vision. The organizers' efforts to incorporate numerous servicing and amusement buildings – either tensile or inflatable – did not achieve the success which was hoped, but the image of a 'temporary city' was achieved.

is there any acknowledgement of the nomadic quality of existence as experienced by almost all students – including students of architecture. In fantasizing *a possible technology for dissent*, the technological superhumanists have seized a unique position as near the centre of contemporary cultural upheaval as was the constructivist architecture of the Russian pioneers to the spirit of revolutionary communism. Like revolutionary communism, 'music in the park' might well harden into an authoritarian, oppressive bureaucracy: alternatively, world events may overtake the peaceful philosophy of itinerancy in the same manner as Nazism overtook the harmless tramping and singing of the *Wandervögel* – the inter-war Hippies of Germany.

Whether this happens or not, there can be little doubt that the *idea* of a nomadic existence, fed and facilitated by equipment derived from automotive models, has potentially enormous support. Not only does it correspond to the life style of a sizable minority of Western youth, but it adumbrates a possible solution to the intolerable problems of organization and administration in our 'tight fit' cities of today. Clanking, mechanical predecessors like the Archigram Computer City, or Cedric Price's 'Potteries Thinkbelt' clearly reveal the organizational advantages of *other directed* mobility: the unique contribution of Webb's and Greene's nomad studies is to restore control of this movement to the individual – and thus shift the philosophical emphasis from totalitarian determinism back to a simulation of the existential plight of man himself. The remaining problem is the integration of this embryonic life style into the complete social context of Western life; into the complex of production, distribution, exploitation and reconciliation that at present enshrouds and conceals 'the housing problem'.

The accusations of irrelevance, utopianism and sheer ignorance of the real housing situation levelled at exponents of collapsible domes, pods, flying houses and megastructures are based on a major misconception which – it must be admitted – derives in part from the inarticulacy and real ignorance of the *avant garde*. The misconception is, of course, the idea that these mutated dwelling forms are intended one day to be financed by a structure similar to that which deals with traditional housing. This is, of course, nonsense. Durability is necessary to act as security for a twenty-, thirty- or sixty-year loan; inflation in land value is necessary to offset the enormous cost of operating at rates of interest of between 8 and 15 per cent. To sacrifice both durability and land value is to write oneself absolutely out of the contemporary housing market – both public and private sector. Thus the deduction of the embattled administrator that technological superhumanism is artistic nonsense, living pods the playthings of rich young trendies who should be occupied with more serious questions.

But here the whole argument can suddenly make a quantum leap: what if the orthodox pattern of housing finance – a house of cards to which additions must be made with infinite care, and from which subtractions are impossible – turned out to be the real nonsense? What if the tightening inflationary spiral, the steeply-climbing land values, the open-ended subsidies, the archaic building methods, the lifetime commitment to a game of value increase, which has few real winners and many losers, merely adds up to a vicious circle from which there can be no escape under the reigning system? There is something about the *effort* that goes into conventional housing, the exhaustion and the continual failure to make real headway, which suggests somehow that we are 'doing it all wrong'. When a thing is as difficult as that there must be an easier way to do it.

Much of the technology envisaged by the technological superhumanists has no links with conventional financing, building legislation or land ownership: its very isolation from these well-established institutions of environmental enterprise guarantees it a future nowhere except somewhere else. Interestingly enough, the escalation to reality

involved in *actually building things* seems not to be the watershed anticipated by critics of the superhumanist school. Archigram, for example, far from descending to the bread-and-butter level of submitting high density housing schemes for orthodox financing, has won its first major job[1] within that very entertainment industry most widely infiltrated by the pop subculture. The construction of pods, domes, tents and inflatables tends by itself to undermine orthodox financing and threatens the status of land values formerly thought inviolate. It is true that the development of such structures is in its infancy and it could hardly be claimed that orthodox building economics are as yet in serious danger; nonetheless, there are straws in the wind. The inflatable office building designed by Norman Foster Associates and erected at Hemel Hempstead outside London in early 1970, encloses 8000 sq. ft of workspace and costs overall about 14s per sq. ft – less than one-tenth the cost of comparable 'heavy' construction. More traditionally in Japan, the whole balance of expenditure between the dwelling enclosure and the range of consumer durables which

1 'Features Monte Carlo', a multi-purpose entertainment enclosure for the foreshore of the Principality at Monaco, was the winner of a £3 million closed competition held in 1969. Construction of the underground complex is scheduled to begin in 1971.

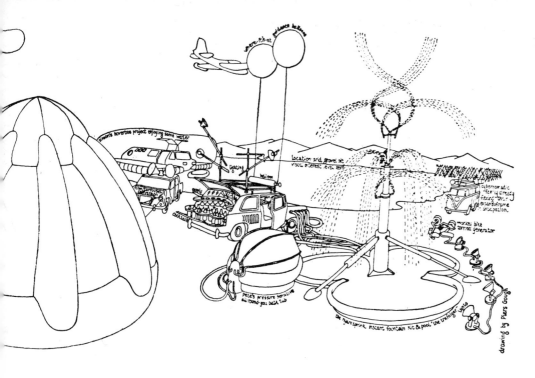

drawing by Piers Gough

go within and without it, represents complete reversal of Western practice. A Japanese family of six will live in a light timber house without internal lavatory or fitted kitchen. They will, however, have a car for each adult male member of the household, numerous television sets, ingenious calor gas powered heating and cooking devices; and a social life involving eating, drinking and bathing in comparative luxury. The actual house enclosure is very cheap and the only service provided in the same manner as the West is electricity. The difference, of course, lies in the more flexible attitude to environment adopted by the commercially oriented computer firm who commissioned Foster's inflatable; and the wholly different social traditions of the Japanese. Lightweight, short-life structures can make sense in an economic context built around them – or *within which they are built*. In the context of an inflationary spiral sufficiently alarming to discourage reasoned thought, they can make little headway. Thus to see how the traditional concept of housing can be modified or *unwound*, we must look to those social groups which are devel-oping life styles *outside* the conventional spiral.

These groups tend to be young, but are not exclusively so. Only those free from a lifetime's commitment to purchase or rental are really capable of experimenting with lifestyles at all – and, in the West, the largest group of such people is to be found in the 15–25 age group. The execration with which the experiments of these people are greeted by the silent majority of Western middle-class societies should be a sufficient clue to the perceptive as to their ultimate importance. As Henry James once observed, a new idea goes through three basic stages of recognition. First it is rejected with contempt, then derided as trivial; finally, it is universally accepted as so important that its very opponents claim to have invented it themselves. It is my belief that the unworkability of conventional housing finance will soon bring about the third phase of James' triad. Within a decade we should see a radical change in housing policy in the West – and one which owes little or nothing to the time-honoured principle of permanence.

123

Bibliography

The coming of mass housing

Barley, M. W. *The House and Home* Vista Books, London 1963

Chadwick, Edwin Sanitary conditions of the Labouring population in England, Aldine 1942

Honikman, Basil 'Port Sunlight and the Garden City Movement' *Systems, Building and Design* October 1968

Jekyll, G. and **S. R. Jones** *Old English Household Life* Batsford, London 1939

McAllister, G. and **E. G.** *Town and Country Planning* Faber and Faber, London 1941

Morley, J. *Life of Richard Cobden* T. Fisher Unwin, London 1881

Report of the Royal Commission Examining the condition of the Urban Poor, London 1887

Seebohm Committee Report on the organisation and responsibilities of the local authority personal social services in England and Wales, London 1968

Tarn, John Nelson 'Some Pioneer Housing Estates' *Architectural Review* May 1968

The birth of the public sector

Banham, Reyner P. *Theory and Design in the First Machine Age* Architectural Press, London 1960

Bertram, Anthony *Design* Penguin Books, London 1938

Conrads, Ulrich and **Hans Sperlich** *Fantastic Architecture* Architectural Press, London 1963; *Architecture of Fantasy*, Praeger, New York 1963

Donnison, D. V. *The Government of Housing* Penguin Books, London 1967

Engels, F. *The Housing Question* Lawrence and Wishart, London 1936

Gallion, A. B. and **Simon Eisner** *The Urban Pattern* D. Van Nostrand, New York 1950

Lubetkin, Berthold 'Town and Landscape Planning in Soviet Russia' *The Architectural Association Journal* January 1933

McAllister, G. and **E. G.** *Town and Country Planning* Faber and Faber, London 1941

Miller Lane, Barbara *Architecture and Politics in Germany 1918 – 1945* Harvard University Press, Cambridge, Mass. 1968

Tudor-Walters Committee Report, London 1918

Yorke, F. R. S. *The Modern House* Architectural Press, London 1934

The Depression and after

Banham, Reyner, Peter Hall and **Paul Barker** 'Non-plan' *New Society*, London, 21 March 1969

Barker, Roger and **Herbert Wright** 'Psychological Ecology and the Problem of Psycho-Social Development' *Child Development* vol 20, no 3, September 1949

Bertram, Anthony *Design* Penguin Books, London 1938

Boudon, Philippe *Pessac de Le Corbusier* Editions Dunod, Paris 1969

Cowburn, William 'Popular Housing' *Architectural Association Journal*, London, October 1966

Daley, Janet 'The Myth of Quantifiability' *Architects' Journal*, 21 August 1968

Donnison, D. V. *The Government of Housing* Penguin Books, London 1967

Douhet, Guilio *Command of the Air* Coward McCann, New York 1942

Everybody's Book of Politics Odhams, London 1937

Fry, Maxwell E. *Fine Building* Faber, London 1944

Gallion, A. B. and **Simon Eisner** *The Urban Pattern* D. Van Nostrand, New York 1950, 2nd ed. 1963

Goff, Bruce (Special Issue) *Architectural Design*, May 1957

Gropius, Walter *The Scope of Total Architecture* George Allen and Unwin, London 1956; Collier Macmillan, New York 1962

Habraken, N. J. *De Dragers en de Mensen* Scheltema and Holkema, Amsterdam 1961

Hole, W. V. 'User Needs and the Design of Houses – the current and potential contribution of social studies' CIB Commission W45, Symposium proceedings of October 1967. Published by the Swedish Institute for Building Research, Stockholm 1967

Homes for Today and Tomorrow report of a subcommittee of the Central Housing Advisory Committee, HMSO, London 1961

'Housing and Environment' (Special issue) *Architectural Review*, Nov 1967

International Unemployment: a study of fluctuations in employment and unemployment in several countries 1910–1930 International Institute of Industrial Relations (IRI), The Hague 1932

Kelly Smith, Norris *Frank Lloyd Wright: a study in architectural content* Prentice-Hall, New York 1966

Lubetkin, Berthold 'Town and Landscape Planning in Soviet Russia' *The Architectural Association Journal* January 1933

McAllister, G. and **E. G.** *Town and Country Planning* Faber and Faber, London 1941

M'Gonigle, G. C. M. and **J. Kirby** *Poverty and Public Health* Gollancz, London 1936

Mailer, Norman *Moonshot* Weidenfeld and Nicolson, London 1970

Miller Lane, Barbara *Architecture and Politics in Germany 1918–1945* Harvard University Press, Cambridge, Mass. 1968

Noble, John 'Appraisal of User Requirements in Mass Housing' *Architects' Journal* 24 August 1966

Noble, John 'The How and Why of Behaviour: Social Psychology for the Architect' *Architects' Journal*, 1963. *137*

Report of the Royal Commission on the Distribution of Industrial Population Cmnd. 6153 (HMSO) London 1940. (The Barlow Report)

Yorke, F. R. S. *The Modern House* Architectural Press, London 1934

Ward, Anthony 'Right and Wrong' *Architectural Design*, July 1969

Wood, C. Leslie *As You Were* W. L. Clifford and Co., London 1936

Bombers are a plan's best friend

Bramsted, Ernest K. *Goebbels and National Socialist Propaganda 1925–1945* The Cresset Press, London 1965; Michigan State University Press, Michigan 1965

Donnison, D. V. *The Government of Housing* Penguin Books, London 1967

Fry, Maxwell E. *Fine Building* Faber and Faber, London 1944

Gropius, Walter *The New Architecture and the Bauhaus* Faber and Faber, London 1935; MIT Press, Cambridge Mass.

Irving, David *The Destruction of Dresden* William Kimber, London 1963; Ballentine Books, New York

Le Corbusier *Towards a New Architecture* Architectural Press, London 1927; Praeger, New York 1969

McAllister, G. and **E. G.** *Town and Country Planning* Faber and Faber, London 1941

McHale, John. R. *Buckminster Fuller* Prentice-Hall International, London 1962

Madge, John (ed) *Tomorrow's Houses* Pilot Press, London 1946

Miller Lane, Barbara *Architecture and Politics in Germany 1918–1945* Harvard University Press, Cambridge Mass. 1968

Sheppard, Richard *Prefabrication in Building* Architectural Press, London 1946

Tetlow, John and **Anthony Goss** *Homes, Towns and Traffic* Faber and Faber, London 1965; Praeger, New York 1968

When We Build Again Bournville Village Trust, Allen and Unwin, London 1941

The end of the strategic argument

Abrams, Charles *Housing in the Modern World* Faber and Faber, London 1966

Burchard, J. *The Voice of the Phoenix: post-war architecture in Germany* Massachusetts Institute of Technology Press, Cambridge, Mass. 1966

Cleeve Barr, A. W. *Public Authority Housing* Batsford, London 1958

Donnison, D. V. *The Government of Housing* Penguin Books, London 1967

Gallion, A. B. and **Simon Eisner** *The Urban Pattern* D. Van Nostrand, New York 1950

Harrington, Michael *The Other America* Penguin Books, London 1963; Macmillan, New York 1962

Kidder Smith, G. E. *The New Architecture of Europe* Penguin Books, London 1961

Osborn, Frederic and **Arnold Whittick** *The New Towns* Leonard Hill, London 1963

Breakdown of a theory

Abrams, Charles *Housing in the Modern World* Faber and Faber, London 1966

Evaluation Project of the Superblocks of the Banco Obrero in Venezuela United Nations Publications 1959

Lipman, Alan 'The Architectural Belief System and Social Behaviour' *British Journal of Sociology*, London 1968

No exit

Bombard, Alain *Naufrage Volontaire* Editions de Paris 1953

Gray, Hamish *The Cost of Council Housing* Institute of Economic Affairs, London 1968

Laing, R. D. *The Divided Self* Penguin Books London 1965

Lèvi-Strauss, Claude *The Savage Mind* Weidenfeld & Nicolson, London 1966; University of Chicago Press, Chicago 1966

Manton, Michael 'The Architecture of Advertising' *Architectural Association Journal* London, 1968

Old Houses into New Homes HMSO, London 1968

Searles, Harold *The Nonhuman Environment* International Universities Press, New York 1960

New directions

Archigram I 'A Statement of the Standpoint of the New Generation' London May 1961

Archigram 5 'Metropolis' London, September 1964

Black, Stephen *Man and Motor Cars* Secker and Warburg, London 1964; Norton, New York 1967

Banham, Reyner P. 'A Home is not a House' *Art in America*, April 1965

Donnison, D. V. *The Government of Housing* Penguin Books, London 1967

Habraken, N. J. *De Dragers en de Mensen* Scheltema and Holkema, Amsterdam 1961

March, Lionel 'Towards a Garden of Cities' *The Listener*, London, 21 March 1968.

Rapoport, Amos *House Form and Culture* Prentice-Hall, London and New York 1969

Stein, Clarence *Toward New Towns for America* MIT Press 1928

Tetlow, John and **Anthony Goss** *Homes Towns and Traffic* Faber and Faber London 1965; Praeger, New York 1968

White, R. B. 'Prefabrication – past, present and potential' *RIBA Journal* September 1962

Photo-acknowledgements

Publisher and author would like to thank the following for their permission to use photographs in this book: Aerofilms 14, 15, 31, 84; Archigram 95–100; *Architects' Journal* (redrawn) 78; Architectural Association 30, 45; Architectural Press 32; *Architecture d'Aujourdhui* 20, 26; Archivbild des Stadtischen, Hannover 63; Associated Press 51; Barley, M. W. 3; Beaudoin 28; Boudon, Philippe 79–82; Braithwaites 54; British Museum 6; Buchanan, J. 94; Burnet, Sir J. 33, 34; Camera Press 11 (Photo Lensart), 19, 38, 42, 43, 52, 58, 59, 62, 68 (Photo Tass), 69 (Photo Tass), 75 (Photo Tom Blau), 77 (Photo Malcolm Pendrill), 87 & 88 (Photo Malcolm Pendrill), 90, 92 (Photo John Gittens: Pix), 93 (Photo Hollywood Press Syndicate); Central Press Photos Ltd 39; Collischonn, H., Frankfurt 21; Cook, P. 102; Cowburn, W. 89; Dell, Simon, 4, 29; Fox Photos Ltd 37; Gallion and Eisner (redrawn) 22, 56; Herein, J. 72, 73; Hervé, L. 25, 83; *L'Illustration* 17; Jol, Gaston Le *Grandes constructions a loyers economiques* ed C. Massin 16; Keystone Press 66; Landesbildstelle, Württemberg 26; Lambert, Sam 67; Leco Photo Service NY 44, 55; Lincoln, Andrew 76; London News Agencies 86; Manx Museum 1; Mart Stam Exhibition 27; National Monuments Record 2, 5, 10; Oxford Press Photography 91; Planet News 53; Radio Times Hulton Picture Library 7, 9; Rowntree Trust, Birmingham 8, 18; Schwab, Gerhard, Stuttgart 69; Tentest Fibre Board Company 74; Topical Press 50, 57, 65; Topix 101; United States Information Service 70, 71; and Verband Berliner Wohningsbau 23.

Index